Where do I go for answ

What's the best and easiest way to plan and book my trip?

frommers.travelocity.com

Frommer's, the travel guide leader, has teamed up with **Travelocity.com,** the leader in online travel, to bring you an in-depth, easy-to-use resource designed to help you plan and book your trip online.

At **frommers.travelocity.com**, you'll find free online updates about your destination from the experts at Frommer's plus the outstanding travel planning and purchasing features of Travelocity.com. Travelocity.com provides reservations capabilities for 95 percent of all airline seats sold, more than 47,000 hotels, and over 50 car rental companies. In addition, Travelocity.com offers more than 2,000 exciting vacation and cruise packages. Travelocity.com puts you in complete control of your travel planning with these and other great features:

> **Expert travel guidance from Frommer's** - over 150 writers reporting from around the world!

> **Best Fare Finder** - an interactive calendar tells you when to travel to get the best airfare

> **Fare Watcher** - we'll track airfare changes to your favorite destinations

> **Dream Maps** - a mapping feature that suggests travel opportunities based on your budget

> **Shop Safe Guarantee** - 24 hours a day / 7 days a week live customer service, and more!

Whether traveling on a tight budget, looking for a quick weekend getaway, or planning the trip of a lifetime, Frommer's guides and Travelocity.com will make your travel dreams a reality. You've bought the book, now book the trip!

A New Star-Rating System
& Other Exciting News
from Frommer's!

In our continuing effort to publish the savviest, most up-to-date, and most appealing travel guides available, we've added some great new features.

Frommer's guides now include a new **star-rating system.** Every hotel, restaurant, and attraction is rated from 0 to 3 stars to help you set priorities and organize your time.

We've also added **seven brand-new features** that point you to the great deals, in-the-know advice, and unique experiences that separate travelers from tourists. Throughout the guide look for:

Finds	Special finds—those places only insiders know about
Fun Fact	Fun facts—details that make travelers more informed and their trips more fun
Kids	Best bets for kids—advice for the whole family
Moments	Special moments—those experiences that memories are made of
Overrated	Places or experiences not worth your time or money
Tips	Insider tips—some great ways to save time and money
Value	Great values—where to get the best deals

Frommer's®

PORTABLE

Charleston & Savannah

4th Edition

by Darwin Porter & Danforth Prince

Hungry Minds™

Best-Selling Books • Digital Downloads • e-Books
Answer Networks • e-Newsletters • Branded Web Sites • e-Learning
New York, NY • Cleveland, OH • Indianapolis, IN

ABOUT THE AUTHOR

A North Carolina native, **Darwin Porter** has lived in South Carolina and Georgia and explored extensively in the region's major cities and backwoods hamlets. He was a bureau chief of the *Miami Herald* at age 21 and has written numerous best-selling Frommer's guides, notably to France, England, Italy, and the Caribbean. He is the coauthor of *Frommer's The Carolinas & Georgia,* working with **Danforth Prince,** formerly of the Paris bureau of the *New York Times*. Dan has lived in Georgia and traveled extensively in the tri-state area.

Published by:

HUNGRY MINDS, INC.

909 Third Ave.
New York, NY 10022

ISBN 0-7645-6558-3
ISSN 1090-154X

Editor: Alexis Flippin
Production Editor: M. Faunette Johnston
Cartographer: John Decamillis
Photo Editor: Richard Fox
Production by Hungry Minds Indianapolis Production Services

SPECIAL SALES

For general information on Hungry Minds' products and services, please contact our Customer Care department; within the U.S. at 800-762-2974, outside the U.S. at 317-572-3993 or fax 317-572-4002. For sales inquiries and reseller information, including discounts, bulk sales, customized editions, and premium sales, please contact our Customer Care department at 800-434-3422.

Manufactured in the United States of America

5   4   3   2   1

Contents

List of Maps

AN INVITATION TO THE READER

In researching this book, we discovered many wonderful places—hotels, restaurants, shops, and more. We're sure you'll find others. Please tell us about them, so we can share the information with your fellow travelers in upcoming editions. If you were disappointed with a recommendation, we'd love to know that, too. Please write to:

Frommer's Portable Charleston & Savannah, 4th Edition
Hungry Minds, Inc. • 909 Third Ave. • New York, NY 10022

AN ADDITIONAL NOTE

Please be advised that travel information is subject to change at any time—and this is especially true of prices. We therefore suggest that you write or call ahead for confirmation when making your travel plans. The authors, editors, and publisher cannot be held responsible for the experiences of readers while traveling. Your safety is important to us, however, so we encourage you to stay alert and be aware of your surroundings. Keep a close eye on cameras, purses, and wallets, all favorite targets of thieves and pickpockets.

WHAT THE SYMBOLS MEAN

The following abbreviations are used for credit cards:

AE	American Express	DISC	Discover
DC	Diners Club	MC	MasterCard	V	Visa

FROMMERS.COM

Now that you have the guidebook to a great trip, visit our website at **www.frommers.com** for travel information on nearly 2,000 destinations. With features updated regularly, we give you instant access to the most current trip-planning information available. At Frommers.com, you'll also find the best prices on airfares, accommodations, and car rentals—and you can even book travel online through our travel booking partners. At Frommers.com, you'll also find the following:

- Daily Newsletter highlighting the best travel deals
- Hot Spot of the Month/Vacation Sweepstakes & Travel Photo Contest
- More than 200 Travel Message Boards
- Outspoken Newsletters and Feature Articles on travel bargains, vacation ideas, tips and resources, and more!

Planning Your Trip to Charleston & Savannah

This chapter is designed to provide most of the nuts-and-bolts travel information you'll need before you set off for South Carolina or Georgia. Browse through this section before you hit the road to ensure that you've touched all the bases.

1 Visitor Information & Money

VISITOR INFORMATION

IN SOUTH CAROLINA Before leaving home, write or call ahead for specific information on sports and sightseeing. Contact **South Carolina Division of Tourism,** 1205 Pendleton St. (P.O. Box 71), Columbia, SC 29202 (© 803/734-0122; fax 803/734-0133; www.travelsc.com). It can also furnish *South Carolina: Smiling Faces, Beautiful Places,* a detailed booklet with photos that covers each region of the state.

When you enter South Carolina, look for one of the 10 **travel information centers** located on virtually every major highway near the border with neighboring states. Information sources for specific destinations are listed in the chapters that follow.

IN GEORGIA For advance reading and planning, contact the **Division of Tourism,** Georgia Department of Industry, Trade & Tourism, P.O. Box 1776, Atlanta, GA 30301-1776 (© 800/VISIT-GA or 404/656-3590; www.gomm.com). Ask for information on your specific interests, as well as a calendar of events (Jan–June or July–Dec).

State Information Centers are located near Atlanta, Augusta, Columbus, Kingsland, Lavonia, Plains, Ringgold, Savannah, Sylvania, Tallapoosa, Valdosta, and West Point. They're open Monday to Saturday from 9am to 6pm and on Sunday from noon to 6pm. Information sources for specific destinations are listed in the chapters that follow.

A particularly useful web resource for travel information for both locations is **CityNet** (www.city.net), which provides links organized by location, then by category, to hundreds of other sites throughout the Internet.

2 When to Go

CLIMATE

This is a mighty hot and steamy part of the country in summer—it's incredibly humid in July and August (sometimes in June and September as well). But temperatures are never extreme the rest of the year, as shown in the average highs and lows noted in the charts below. Winter temperatures seldom drop below freezing anywhere in the state. Spring and fall are the longest seasons, and the wettest months are December to April.

Spring, which usually begins in March, is just spectacular. Delicate pink and white dogwoods and azaleas in vivid shades burst into brilliant bloom. Both Charleston and Savannah are heaven for gardeners (or anyone who likes to stop and smell the roses), so March and April are memorable times to visit. In the springtime and during Charleston's Spoleto Festival (see the Calendar of Events, below), hotel prices rise and reservations are hard to come by.

Charleston Average Temperatures & Rainfall

	Jan	Feb	Mar	Apr	May	June	July	Aug	Sept	Oct	Nov	Dec
High (°F)	59	61	68	76	83	87	89	89	85	77	69	61
Low (°F)	40	41	48	56	64	70	74	74	69	49	49	42
Rain (in.)	3.5	3.3	4.3	2.7	4.0	6.4	6.8	7.2	4.7	2.9	2.5	3.2

Savannah Average Temperatures & Rainfall

	Jan	Feb	Mar	Apr	May	June	July	Aug	Sept	Oct	Nov	Dec
High (°F)	60	62	70	78	84	89	91	90	85	78	70	62
Low (°F)	38	41	48	55	63	69	72	72	68	57	57	41
Rain (in.)	3.6	3.2	3.8	3.0	4.1	5.7	6.4	7.5	4.5	2.4	2.2	3.0

CHARLESTON, HILTON HEAD & SAVANNAH CALENDAR OF EVENTS

January

Low-Country Oyster Festival, Charleston. Steamed buckets of oysters greet visitors at Boone Hall Plantation. Enjoy live music, oyster-shucking contests, children's events, and various other

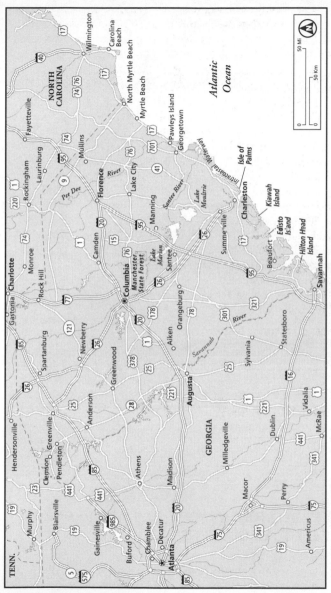

activities. Contact the Greater Charleston Restaurant Association at © **843/577-4030.** End of January.

February

Wormsloe Celebrates the Founding of Georgia, Savannah. Wormsloe was the colonial fortified home of Noble Jones, one of Georgia's first colonists. Costumed demonstrators portray skills used by those early settlers. Tickets cost $2 for adults and $1 for children. Call © **912/353-3023.** Early February.

Southeastern Wildlife Exposition, Charleston. More than 150 of the finest artists and more than 500 exhibitors participate at 13 locations in the downtown area. Enjoy carvings, sculpture, paintings, live-animal exhibits, food, and much more. Call © **843/723-1748** for details (www.sew.com). Mid-February.

Savannah Irish Festival, Savannah. This Irish heritage celebration promises fun for the entire family, with music, dancing, and food. There's both a children's stage and a main stage. Contact the Irish Committee of Savannah at © **912/234-8444.** Mid-February.

March

St. Patrick's Day Celebration on the River, Savannah. The river flows green and so does the beer in one of the largest celebrations held on River Street each year. Enjoy live entertainment, lots of food, and tons of fun. Contact the Savannah Waterfront Association at © **912/234-0295.** St. Patrick's Day weekend.

Festival of Houses and Gardens, Charleston. For nearly 50 years, people have been enjoying some of Charleston's most historic neighborhoods and private gardens on this tour. Contact the Historic Charleston Foundation, P.O. Box 1120, Charleston, SC 29402 (© **848/724-8481**) for details. Mid-March to mid-April.

Family Circle Magazine Cup, Hilton Head Island. This $750,000 tournament brings the best women's tennis players to the island. Call © **843/363-3500** for details. Late March to early April.

April

Cooper River Bridge Run. Sponsored by the Medical University of South Carolina, this run and walk starts in Mt. Pleasant, goes over the Cooper River, and ends in the center of Charleston. For information, call © **843/722-3405.** April 1.

MCI Classic, Hilton Head. This $1.3-million tournament brings an outstanding field of PGA tour professionals to this event each year. The weeklong tournament is held at Harbour Town Golf Links in Sea Pines Plantation. Contact Classic Sports, Inc., 71 Lighthouse Rd., Suite 414, Hilton Head, SC 29928 (© **843/671-2448**). Mid-April.

TENNESSEE

Knoxville

NORTH CAROLINA

Chattanooga

Charlotte

Blairsville
Chattahoochee
National Forest

Greenville

SOUTH
CAROLINA

Dahlonega

Calhoun

Gainesville

Columbia

Cartersville

Lake
Sidney
Lanier

Athens

Chamblee
Atlanta
Decatur

Georgia's Stone
Mountain Park

Clarks Hill
Lake

Washington

Madison

Augusta

Crawfordville

Eatonton

Lake
Sinclair

Milledgeville

Callaway
Gardens

Macon

Sylvania

Warm
Springs

Dublin

Columbus

Perry

ALABAMA

Americus

Vidalia

Plains

McRae

Savannah

Albany

Jesup

Statesboro

The Golden Isles

Dothan

Waycross

Lake
Seminole

Bainbridge

Thomasville

Valdosta

Waycross
State Forest

Okefenokee
Swamp
Park

Atlantic
Ocean

Tallahassee

Jacksonville

Panama City

FLORIDA

Gulf of Mexico

0   50 Mi
0   50 Km

May

American Classic Tea Open House, Charleston. America's only tea plantation takes you on a free historical tour. Don't forget to buy some great blends when you leave. Contact the Charleston Tea Plantation at © **843/559-0383.** Early May.

Savannah Symphony Duck Race, Savannah. Each year the Savannah Symphony Women's Guild plays host as a flock of rubber ducks hits the water to go with the flow of the tides along Savannah's historic River Street. There's a $5,000 grand prize for the winning ducky. All proceeds benefit the Savanah Symphony. Call © **912/236-9536.** Early May.

Memorial Day at Old Fort Jackson, Savannah. The ceremonies have a flag-raising ceremony and a memorial service. Contact the Coastal Heritage Society at © **912/232-3945.** Late May.

Spoleto Festival U.S.A., Charleston. This is the premier cultural event in the tri-state area. This famous international festival—the American counterpart of the equally celebrated one in Spoleto, Italy—showcases world-renowned performers in drama, dance, music, and art in various venues throughout the city. For details and this year's schedule, contact Spoleto Festival U.S.A., P.O. Box 157, Charleston, SC 29402 (© **843/722-2764;** www.spoleto usa.org). Late May through early June.

June

Juneteenth, Savannah. This event highlights the contributions of more than 200,000 African Americans who fought for their freedom and that of future generations. This event is a celebration of the Emancipation Proclamation. Although this promise of freedom was announced in January, it was not until the middle of June (actual date unknown) that the news reached Savannah, thus prompting the remembrance of "Juneteenth." For more information, contact the Coastal Heritage Society at © **912/ 651-6840.** Mid-June.

August

The Taste of Charleston!, Charleston. This annual event offers an afternoon of food, fun, entertainment, and more. Charleston's best restaurants offer their specialties in bite-size portions, so you can sample all of them. For more information, call © **843/ 577-4030.** In 2002, August 31 and September 1.

September

Savannah Jazz Festival, Savannah. This festival features national and local jazz and blues legends. A jazz brunch and music at different venues throughout the city are among the highlights. Contact Host South at ✆ **912/232-2222.** Mid-September.

Scottish Games and Highland Gathering, Charleston. This gathering of Scottish clans features medieval games, bagpipe performances, Scottish dancing, and other traditional activities. Call The Scottish Society of Charleston at ✆ **843/556-2417.** Mid-September.

Candelight Tour of Houses & Gardens, Charleston. Sponsored by the Preservation Society of Charleston, this annual event provides an intimate look at many of the area's historic homes, gardens, and churches. For more information, call ✆ **843/ 7222-4630.** September 22 to October 28.

October

MOJA Festival, Charleston. Celebrating the rich African-American heritage in the Charleston area, this festival features lectures, art exhibits, stage performances, historical tours, concerts, and much more. Contact the Charleston Office of Cultural Affairs at ✆ **843/724-7305.** Early October.

Fall Tour of Homes, Beaufort. Frank Lloyd Wright's Aldbrass Plantation is only one of the beautiful homes on this tour. The public is invited to get a rare view of this coastal city's most stately residences during a 3-day tour. Call ✆ **843/524-6334;** www.beaufortonline.com. Mid-October.

November

Crafts Festival and Cane Grinding, Savannah. More than 75 craft artists from four states sell and demonstrate their art. Music is provided by the Savannah Folk Music Society. Contact Oatland Island at ✆ **912/897-3773.** Mid-November.

December

Christmas in Charleston, Charleston. This month-long celebration features home and church tours, Christmas-tree lightings, craft shows, artistry, and a peek at how Old Charleston celebrated the holiday season. For more information on how to participate or to visit. Call ✆ **800/868-8118.** December 1 to 31.

Christmas 1864, Savannah. Fort Jackson hosts the dramatic re-creation of its evacuation on December 20, 1864. More than 60 Civil War reenactors play the part of Fort Jackson's Confederate defenders, who were preparing to evacuate ahead of Union Gen. William Tecumseh Sherman. Contact Old Fort Jackson at ✆ **912/232-3945.** Early December.

Annual Holiday Tour of Homes, Savannah. The doors of Savannah's historic homes are opened to the public in the holiday season. Each home is decorated, and a different group of homes is shown every day. Contact the Downtown Neighborhood Association at ℂ **912/236-8362.** Mid-December.

3 Tips for Travelers with Special Needs

This section provides a wealth of invaluable resources for travelers with special needs.

FOR TRAVELERS WITH DISABILITIES   The State of South Carolina has numerous agencies that assist people with disabilities. For specific information, call the **South Carolina Handicapped Services Information System** (ℂ **803/777-5732**). Two other agencies that may prove to be helpful are the **South Carolina Protection & Advocacy System for the Handicapped** (ℂ **803/782-0639**) and the **Commission for the Blind** (ℂ **803/734-7520**).

Many hotels and restaurants in Georgia provide easy access for persons with disabilities, and some display the international wheelchair symbol in their brochures. However, it's always a good idea to call ahead. The **Georgia Governor's Developmental Disabilities Council** (ℂ **404/657-2126**) may also be of help. The Georgia Department of Industry, Trade & Tourism publishes a guide, *Georgia on My Mind,* that lists attractions and accommodations with access for persons with disabilities. To receive a copy, contact **Tour Georgia,** P.O. Box 1776, Atlanta, GA 30301 (ℂ **800/VISIT-GA,** ext. 1903).

Many agencies provide advance data to help you plan your trip. One such agency is **Travel Information Service,** Industrial Rehab Program, 1200 W. Tabor Rd., Philadelphia, PA 19141 (ℂ **215/456-9603** or 215/456-9602 for TTY). Another agency is **Mobility International USA,** P.O. Box 10767, Eugene, OR 97440 (ℂ **503/343-1284**). It answers questions on various destinations and also offers discounts on videos, publications, and programs that it sponsors. For a free copy of *Air Transportation of Handicapped Persons,* published by the U.S. Department of Transportation, write for Free Advisory Circular No. AC12032, Distribution Unit, U.S. Department of Transportation, Publications Division, M-4332, Washington, DC 20590.

FOR GAY & LESBIAN TRAVELERS   Gay hot lines in Charleston fall under the 24-hour crisis-prevention network (ℂ **803/744-4357**). Gay hot lines in Columbia are designated as the GLPM hot line (ℂ **803/771-7713**).

The most important information center in the state is the **South Carolina Pride Center,** 1108 Woodrow St., Columbia (℗ **803/ 771-7713**). It's open on Wednesday and Sunday from 1 to 6pm, on Friday from 7 to 11pm, and on Saturday from 1 to 8pm. On the premises are a library, archives, a "gay pride" shop, an inventory of films, and meeting space. It also functions as a conduit for such other organizations as the **Low Country Gay and Lesbian Alliance** (℗ **843/720-8088**).

The free *Etcetera* magazine is offered in virtually every gay-owned or gay-friendly bar, bookstore, and restaurant in the Deep South. It boasts a bona fide circulation of 22,000 readers a week, a figure qualifying it as the largest gay and lesbian publication in the Southeast. If you'd like a copy in advance of your trip, send $2 for a current issue to 151 Renaissance Pkwy., Atlanta, GA 30308.

Another gay publication is *Southern Voice*. Call ℗ **404/876-1819** for information about distribution points throughout the South.

4 Getting There & Getting Around

BY PLANE   You can fly into Charleston on **Continental Airlines** (℗ **800/525-0280;** www.continental.com), **Delta Air Lines** (℗ **800/221-1212;** www.delta.com), **United Airlines** and United Express (℗ **800/241-6522;** www.ual.com), and **US Airways** (℗ **800/428-4322;** www.usairways.com); the major airlines serving South Carolina.

If you're traveling to **Hilton Head,** you have the option of flying US Airways directly to the island or flying into the Savannah (Georgia) International Airport via Continental or Delta and then driving or taking a limousine to Hilton Head, which is 1 hour away.

Virtually every major national airline flies through Atlanta's **Hartsfield International Airport,** 13 miles south of downtown off I-85 and I-285. From Atlanta, there are connecting flights to points around the state, including Savannah. Delta Air Lines is the major carrier to Atlanta, connecting it to pretty much the entire country as well as 32 countries internationally. Delta, United, US Airways, and **American Airlines** (℗ **800/433-7300;** www.aa.com) all serve Savannah's airport.

BY CAR   South Carolina has a network of exceptionally good roads. Interstate 95 enters South Carolina from the north near Dillon and runs straight through the state to Hardeeville on the Georgia border. The major east-west artery is I-26, running from

Charleston northwest through Columbia and on up to Hendersonville, North Carolina. U.S. 17 runs along the coast.

South Carolina furnishes excellent travel information to motorists, and there are well-equipped, efficiently staffed visitor centers at the state border on most major highways. If you have a cell phone in your car and need help, dial ***HP** for Highway Patrol Assistance.

Georgia is crisscrossed by major interstate highways: I-75 bisects the state from Dalton in the north to Valdosta in the south; I-95 runs north-south along the eastern seaboard. The major east-west routes are I-16, running between Macon and Savannah; and I-20, running from Augusta through Atlanta and into Alabama. I-85 runs northeast-southwest in the northern half of the state. The state-run welcome centers at all major points of entry that are staffed with knowledgeable, helpful Georgians who can often advise you as to timesaving routes. The speed limit of 55 miles per hour and the seat-belt law are strictly enforced.

Before you leave home, it's a good idea to join **American Automobile Association** (AAA), 12600 Fairlake Circle, Fairfax, VA 22033-4904 (© **703/222-6000**). For a very small fee, the association provides a wide variety of services, including trip planning and a 24-hour toll-free phone number (© **800/222-4357**) set up exclusively to deal with members' road emergencies.

Leading car-rental firms are represented in both cities and at the airports. For reservations and rate information, call **Avis** (© **800/331-1212**); Budget (© **800/527-0700**); **Hertz** (© **800/654-3131**); or **Thrifty** (© **800/367-2277**).

BY TRAIN   Amtrak (© **800/USA-RAIL**) services both Charleston and Savannah. Amtrak also has tour packages that include hotel, breakfast, and historic-site tours in Charleston at bargain rates. Bargain fares are sometimes in effect for limited periods; you should always check for the most economical way to schedule your trip. Be sure to ask about Amtrak's moneysaving "All Aboard America" regional fares or any other current fare specials. Amtrak also offers attractively priced rail-drive packages in the Carolinas and Georgia.

PACKAGE TOURS   Collette Tours (© **401/728-3805** or 800/832-4656; www.collettetours.com) offers an 8-day fly/drive tour, "Charleston/Myrtle Beach Show Tour" that guides you through a day of Charleston's most historic sites, visits a Civil War–era plantation in Georgetown, and ends up in Myrtle Beach for dinner and entertainment at Dixie Stampede, Broadway at the Beach, and Magic on Ice.

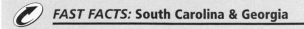

FAST FACTS: South Carolina & Georgia

Area Code It's 843 for Charleston and the South Carolina coast; and 912 for Savannah.

Emergencies Dial ⓒ **911** for police, ambulance, paramedics, and the fire department. You can also dial 0 (zero, *not* the letter *O*) and ask the operator to connect you to emergency services. Travelers Aid can also be helpful; check local telephone directories.

Liquor Laws The minimum drinking age in South Carolina is 21. Some restaurants are licensed to serve only beer and wine, but a great many offer those plus liquor in mini-bottles, which can be added to cocktail mixers. Beer and wine are sold in grocery stores 7 days a week, but all package liquor is offered through local government-controlled stores, commonly called "ABC" (Alcoholic Beverage Control Commission) stores, which are closed on Sundays. In Georgia, if you're 21 or over, you can buy alcoholic beverages in package stores between 8am and midnight (except on Sunday, election days, Thanksgiving, and Christmas).

Newspapers and Magazines The major papers in South Carolina are *The State* (Columbia), the *Greenville News,* and the *Charleston Post and Courier. The Sandlapper* is a local quarterly magazine. The *Atlanta Journal-Constitution* is Georgia's leading daily newspaper. Savannah's leading newspaper is the *Savannah Morning News.*

Taxes South Carolina has a 5% sales tax. Georgia has a 6% sales tax.

Time Zone South Carolina and Georgia are in the Eastern Standard Time zone and go on Daylight Saving Time in summer.

Weather In South Carolina, phone ⓒ **803/822-8135** (www. nws.noaa.gov) for an update. In Georgia, phone ⓒ **900/ 932-8437** (95¢ per minute) for an update.

2

Charleston: Antebellum Grace & Charm

In the closing pages of *Gone With the Wind,* Rhett tells Scarlett that he's going back home to Charleston, where he can find "the calm dignity life can have when it's lived by gentle folks, the genial grace of days that are gone. When I lived those days, I didn't realize the slow charm of them." In spite of all the changes and upheavals over the years, Rhett's endorsement of Charleston still holds true.

If the Old South lives all through South Carolina's Low Country, it positively thrives in Charleston. All our romantic notions of antebellum days—stately homes, courtly manners, gracious hospitality, and above all, gentle dignity—are facts of everyday life in this old city, in spite of a few scoundrels here and there, including an impressive roster of pirates, patriots, and presidents.

Notwithstanding a history dotted with earthquakes, hurricanes, fires, and Yankee bombardments, Charleston remains one of the best-preserved cities in America's Old South. It boasts 73 pre-Revolutionary War buildings, 136 from the late 18th century, and more than 600 built before the 1840s. With its cobblestone streets and horse-drawn carriages, Charleston is a place of visual images and sensory pleasures. Jasmine and wisteria fragrances fill the air; the aroma of she-crab soup (a local favorite) wafts from sidewalk cafes; and antebellum architecture graces the historic cityscape. "No wonder they are so full of themselves," said an envious visitor from Columbia, which may be the state capital but doesn't have Charleston's style and grace.

In its annual reader survey, *Condé Nast Traveler* magazine named Charleston the No. 3 city to visit in America, which places it ahead of such perennial favorites as New York, Seattle, and Santa Fe. Visitors are drawn here from all over the world, and it is now quite common to hear German and French spoken on local streets.

Does this city have a modern side? Yes, but it's well hidden. Chic shops abound, as do a few supermodern hotels, but Charleston has no skyscrapers. You don't come to Charleston for anything cutting-edge, though. You come to glimpse an earlier, almost-forgotten era.

Many local families still own and live in the homes that their planter ancestors built. Charlestonians manage to maintain a way of life that in many respects has little to do with wealth. The simplest encounter with Charleston natives seems to be invested with a social air, as though the visitor were a valued guest. Yet there are those who detect a certain snobbishness in Charleston—and truth be told, you'd have to stay a few hundred years to be considered an insider here.

1 Orientation

ARRIVING

BY PLANE   Charleston International Airport is in North Charleston on I-26, about 12 miles west of the city. Taxi fare into the city runs about $25, and the airport limousine (© **843/767-1100**) has a $20 fare. All major car-rental facilities, including Hertz and Avis, are available at the airport. If you're driving, follow the airport-access road to I-26 into the heart of Charleston.

BY CAR   The main north–south coastal route, U.S. 17, passes through Charleston; I-26 runs northwest to southeast, ending in Charleston. Charleston is 120 miles southeast of Columbia via I-26 and 98 miles south of Myrtle Beach via U.S. 17.

BY TRAIN   Amtrak (© **800/USA-RAIL**) trains arrive at 4565 Gaynor Ave., North Charleston.

VISITOR INFORMATION

Charleston Convention and Visitors Bureau, 375 Meeting St., Charleston, SC 29402 (© **843/853-8000;** www.charlestoncvb.com), just across from the Charleston Museum, provides maps, brochures, tour information, and access to South Carolina Automated Ticketing. The helpful staff will assist you in finding accommodations and planning your stay. Numerous tours depart hourly from the visitors bureau, and restroom facilities, as well as parking, are available. Be sure to allow time to view the 24-minute multi-image presentation "Forever Charleston"; and pick up a copy of the visitor's guide. The center is open from April to October, Monday to Friday from 8:30am to 5:30pm and on Saturday and Sunday from 8am to 5pm; and from November to March daily from 8:30am to 5:30pm.

CITY LAYOUT

Charleston's streets are laid out in an easy-to-follow grid pattern. The main north–south thoroughfares are King, Meeting, and East Bay streets. Tradd, Broad, Queen, and Calhoun streets cross the city from east to west. South of Broad Street, East Bay becomes East Battery.

Unlike most cities, Charleston offers a most helpful map, and it's distributed free. Called **"The Map Guide—Charleston,"** it includes the streets of the historic district as well as surrounding areas, and offers tips on shopping, tours, and what to see and do. Maps are available at the **Visitor Reception & Transportation Center,** 375 Meeting St., at John Street (© **843/853-8000**).

NEIGHBORHOODS IN BRIEF

The Historic District   In 1860, according to one Charlestonian, "South Carolina seceded from the Union, Charleston seceded from South Carolina, and south of Broad Street seceded from Charleston." The city preserves its early years at its southernmost point: the conjunction of the Cooper and Ashley rivers. The White Point Gardens, right in the elbow of the two rivers, provide a sort of gateway into this area, where virtually every home is of historic or architectural interest. Between Broad Street and Murray Boulevard (which runs along the south waterfront), you'll find such sightseeing highlights as St. Michael's Episcopal Church, the Calhoun Mansion, the Edmondston-Alston House, the Old Exchange/Provost Dungeon, the Heyward-Washington House, Catfish Row, and the Nathaniel Russell House.

Downtown   Extending north from Broad Street to Marion Square at the intersection of Calhoun and Meeting streets, this area encloses noteworthy points of interest, good shopping, and a gaggle of historic churches. Just a few of its highlights are the Old City Market, the Dock Street Theatre, Market Hall, the Old Powder Magazine, the Thomas Elfe Workshop, Congregation Beth Elohim, the French Huguenot Church, St. John's Church, and the Unitarian church.

Above Marion Square   The visitor center is located on Meeting Street north of Calhoun. The Charleston Museum is just across the street, and the Aiken-Rhett Mansion, Joseph Manigault Mansion, and Old Citadel are all within easy walking distance in the area bounded by Calhoun Street to the south and Mary Street to the north.

North Charleston Charleston International Airport is at the point where I-26 and I-526 intersect. This makes North Charleston a Low Country transportation hub. Primarily a residential and industrial community, it lacks the charms of the historic district. It's also the home of the North Charleston Coliseum, the largest indoor entertainment venue in South Carolina.

Mount Pleasant East of the Cooper River, just minutes from the heart of the historic district, this community is worth a detour. Filled with accommodations, restaurants, and some attractions, it encloses a historic district along the riverfront known as the Old Village, which is on the National Register's list of buildings. Its major attraction is Patriots Point, the world's largest naval and maritime museum; it's also the home of the aircraft carrier *Yorktown.*

Outlying Areas Within easy reach of the city are Boone Hall Plantation, Fort Moultrie, and the public beaches at Sullivan's Island and Isle of Palms. Head west across the Ashley River Bridge to pay tribute to Charleston's birth at Charles Towne Landing, and visit such highlights as Drayton Hall, Magnolia Gardens, and Middleton Place.

2 Getting Around

BY BUS City bus fares are 75¢, and service is available from 5:35am to 10pm (until 1am to North Charleston). Between 9:30am and 3:30pm, senior citizens and the handicapped pay 25¢. Exact change is required. For route and schedule information, call © **843/ 724-7420.**

BY TROLLEY The **Downtown Area Shuttle (DASH)** is the quickest way to get around the main downtown area daily. The fare is 75¢, and you'll need exact change. A pass that's good for the whole day costs $2. For hours and routes, call © **843/724-7420.**

BY TAXI Leading taxi companies are **Yellow Cab** (© **843/ 577-6565**) and **Safety Cab** (© **843/722-4066**). Each company has its own fare structure. Within the city, however, fares seldom exceed $3 or $4. You must call for a taxi; there are no pickups on the street.

BY CAR If you're staying in the city proper, park your car and save it for day trips to outlying areas. You'll find **parking facilities** scattered about the city, with some of the most convenient at Hutson Street and Calhoun Street, both of which are near Marion

Square; on King Street between Queen and Broad; and on George Street between King and Meeting. If you can't find space on the street to park, the two most centrally located **garages** are on Wentworth Street (© **843/724-7383**) and at Concord and Cumberland (© **843/724-7387**). Charges are $8 all day.

Leading car-rental companies are **Avis Rent-a-Car** (© **800/ 331-1212** or 843/767-7038), **Budget Car and Truck Rentals** (© **800/527-0700;** 843/767-7051 at the airport, 843/760-1410 in North Charleston, or 843/577-5195 downtown), and **Hertz** (© **800/654-3131** or 843/767-4552).

C FAST FACTS: Charleston

American Express The local American Express office is at 956 Provincial Circle, Mt. Pleasant (© **843/881-9339**), open Monday to Friday from 9am to 5pm.

Camera Repair The best option is **Focal Point,** 4 Apollo Rd. (© **843/571-3886**), open Monday to Thursday from 9am to 1pm and 2 to 5pm, and on Friday from 9am to noon.

Car Rentals See "Getting Around," above.

Climate See "When to Go," in chapter 1.

Dentists Consult Orthodontic Associates of Charleston, 86 Rutledge Ave. (© **843/723-7242**).

Doctors For a physician referral or 24-hour emergency-room treatment, contact **Charleston Memorial Hospital,** 326 Calhoun St. (© **843/577-0600**). Another option is **Roper Hospital,** 316 Calhoun St. (© **843/724-2970**). Contact **Doctor's Care** (© **843/556-5585**) for the names of walk-in clinics.

Emergencies In an emergency, dial © **911.** If the situation isn't life-threatening, call © **843/577-7077** for the fire department, © **843/577-7434** for the police, or © **843/747-1888** for an ambulance.

Eyeglass Repair Try **LensCrafters,** 7800 Rivers Ave., North Charleston (© **843/764-3710**), open Monday to Saturday from 10am to 9pm and on Sunday, noon to 6pm.

Hospitals Local hospitals operating 24-hour emergency rooms include **AMI East Cooper Community Hospital,** 1200 Johnnie Dodds Blvd., Mt. Pleasant (© **843/881-0100**); **River Hospital North,** 12750 Spelssegger Dr., North Charleston (© **843/ 744-2110**); **Charleston Memorial Hospital,** 326 Calhoun St.

(© 843/577-0600); and **Medical University of South Carolina,** 171 Ashley Ave. (© 843/792-2300). For medical emergencies, call © **911.**

Hot Lines Crisis Counseling is available at © **800/922-2283** or 843/744-HELP. The Poison Control Center is at © **800/922-1117.**

Newspapers & Magazines *The Post and Courier* is the local daily.

Pharmacies Try **CVS Drugs,** Wanda Crossing, Mt. Pleasant (© **843/881-9435**), open Monday to Saturday from 8am to midnight and on Sunday from 10am to 8pm.

Police Call © **911.** For non-emergency matters, call © **843/ 577-7434.**

Post Office The main post office is at 83 Broad St. (© **843/ 577-0688**), open Monday to Friday from 8:30am to 5:30pm and on Saturday from 9:30am to 2pm.

Restrooms These are available throughout the downtown area, including at Broad and Meeting streets, at Queen and Church streets, on Market Street between Meeting and Church streets, and at other clearly marked strategic points in the historic and downtown districts.

Safety Downtown Charleston is well lighted and patrolled throughout the night to ensure public safety. People can generally walk about downtown at night without fear of violence. Still, after the local trolley system, DASH, closes at 10:30pm, it's wiser to call a taxi than to walk through dark streets.

Taxes A sales tax of 6% is imposed.

Transit Information Contact the Charleston Area Convention Visitor Reception & Transportation Center, 375 Meeting St. (© **843/853-8000**), for information.

Weather Call © **843/744-3207** for an update.

3 Where to Stay

Charleston has many of the best historic inns in America, even surpassing those of Savannah. Hotels and motels are priced in direct ratio to their proximity to the 789-acre historic district; if prices in the center are too high for your budget, find a place west of the Ashley River, and drive into town for sightseeing. In the last decade, the opening and restoration of inns and hotels in Charleston has been phenomenal, although it's slowing somewhat. Charleston ranks among the top cities of America for hotels of charm and character.

Bed-and-breakfast accommodations range from historic homes to carriage houses to simple cottages, and they're located in virtually every section of the city. For details and reservations, contact **Historic Charleston Bed and Breakfast,** 57 Broad St., Charleston, SC 29401 (© **800/743-3583** or 843/722-6606; www. historiccharlestonbedandbreakfast.com). Hours are Monday to Friday 9am to 5pm.

During the Spring Festival of Houses and the Spoleto Festival, rates go up, and owners charge pretty much what the market will bear. Advance reservations are essential at those times.

In a city that has rooms of so many shapes and sizes in the same historic building, classifying hotels by price is difficult. Price often depends on the room itself. Some expensive hotels may in fact have many moderately priced rooms. Moderately priced hotels, on the other hand, may have special rooms that are quite expensive.

When booking a hotel, ask about any package plans that might be available. It pays to ask, because deals come and go; they're most often granted to those who are staying 3 or 4 days.

The down side regarding all these inns of charm and grace is that they are among the most expensive in this guide. Staying in an inn or B&B in the historic district is one of the reasons to go to Charleston, and can do more to evoke the elegance of the city than almost anything else. Innkeepers and B&B owners know this all too well and charge accordingly, especially in the summer season, although winter reductions are common.

If you simply can't afford a stay at one of these historic inns, you can confine your consumption of Charleston to dining in the old city and sightseeing. For many people, that's a satisfying compromise. During the day, you can soak in the glamour of the city, and at night retire to one of the many clean, comfortable—and yes, utterly dull—chain motels on the outskirts. See the most representative samples with names, phone numbers, and rates under our "inexpensive" category, below.

VERY EXPENSIVE

Charleston Place Hotel *✯✯✯*   Charleston's premier hostelry, an Orient Express Property, is an eight-story landmark in the historic

Charleston Accommodations

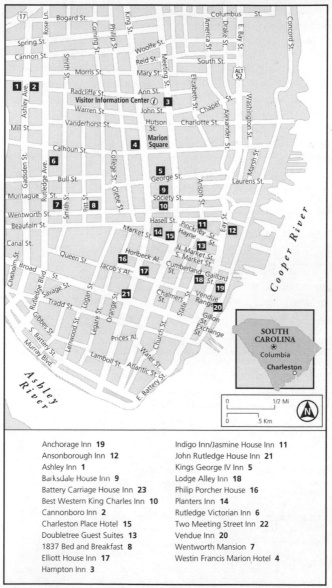

Anchorage Inn **19**
Ansonborough Inn **12**
Ashley Inn **1**
Barksdale House Inn **9**
Battery Carriage House Inn **23**
Best Western King Charles Inn **10**
Cannonboro Inn **2**
Charleston Place Hotel **15**
Doubletree Guest Suites **13**
1837 Bed and Breakfast **8**
Elliott House Inn **17**
Hampton Inn **3**

Indigo Inn/Jasmine House Inn **11**
John Rutledge House Inn **21**
Kings George IV Inn **5**
Lodge Alley Inn **18**
Philip Porcher House **16**
Planters Inn **14**
Rutledge Victorian Inn **6**
Two Meeting Street Inn **22**
Vendue Inn **20**
Wentworth Mansion **7**
Westin Francis Marion Hotel **4**

district that looks like a postmodern French château. It's big-time, uptown, glossy, and urban—at least, a former visitor, Prince Charles, thought so. Governors and prime ministers from around the world, as well as members of Fortune 500 companies, even visiting celebs such as Mel Gibson, prefer to stay here instead at one of the more intimate B&Bs. Bedrooms are among the most spacious and handsomely furnished in town—stately, modern, and maintained in state-of-the-art condition. This hotel represents the New South at its most confident, a stylish giant in a district of B&Bs and small converted inns. Acres of Italian marble grace the place, leading to plush bedrooms with decor inspired by colonial Carolina.

205 Meeting St., Charleston, SC 29401. ℂ **800/611-5545** or 843/722-4900. Fax 843/724-7215. www.charlestonpalacehotel.com. 487 units. $239–$399 double; $500–$1,500 suite. Seasonal packages available. AE, DC, DISC, MC, V. Parking $9. **Amenities:** Deluxe restaurant, Charleston Grill (see "Where to Dine," later in this chapter); café; 24-hour room service; babysitting; laundry; whirlpool; men's steam bath; aerobics studio; sundeck. *In room:* A/C, TV, minibar.

Planters Inn 🐦🐦 *EXCELLENT* For many years, this distinguished brick-sided inn next to the City Market was left to languish. In 1994, a multimillion-dollar renovation transformed the place into a cozy but tasteful and opulent enclave of colonial charm. A member of Relais & Chateaux, the inn has a lobby filled with reproductions of 18th-century furniture and engravings, a staff clad in silk vests, and a parking area with exactly the right amount of spaces for the number of rooms in the hotel. The spacious bedrooms have hardwood floors, marble baths, and 18th-century decor (the work of award-wining decorators). The suites are appealing, outfitted very much like rooms in an upscale private home.

Market and Meeting streets, Charleston, SC 29401. ℂ **800/845-7082** or 843/722-2345. Fax 843/577-2125; www.plantersinn.com. E-mail: reservations@ planterinn.com. 62 units. $185–$300 double; $300–$600 suite. AE, DC, DISC, MC, V. Valet parking $14 a day. **Amenities:** Afternoon tea in the lobby; a well-recommended restaurant, the Peninsula Grill (see "Where to Dine," later in this chapter); same-day laundry and dry cleaning service; concierge; twice-daily maid service; meeting rooms; shopping arcade. Babysitting and massage are available at an additional charge; a health club and bicycle rentals are located nearby. *In room:* A/C, TV, dataport, hair dryer, iron, safe.

Wentworth Mansion 🐦🐦 An example of America's Gilded Age, this 1886 Second Empire Inn touts such amenities as hand-carved marble fireplaces, Tiffany stained-glass windows, and detailed wood and plasterwork. If it is a grand accommodation that you seek, you've found it. When a cotton merchant built the property in the

1800s, it cost $200,000, an astronomical sum back then. In the mid-1990s, a team of local entrepreneurs spent millions renovating it into the smooth and seamless inn you see today. Prior to its reopening in 1998, it had been a rundown office building. The rooms and suites are large enough to have sitting areas. All units have a king-size bed and whirlpool, and most have working gas fireplaces. The mansion rooms and suites also come with a sleeper sofa for extra guests, who are charged an additional $50 per night.

149 Wentworth St., Charleston, SC 29401. © **888/466-1886** or 843/853-1886. Fax 843/720-5290 www.wentworthmansion.com. E-mail: wentworthmansion@ aol.com. 21 units. $225–$415 double, $395–$695 suite. Rates include breakfast buffet and evening tea. AE, DC, DISC, MC, V. Free parking. **Amenities:** Circa 1886 Restaurant (see "Where to Dine," later in this chapter); continental breakfast served in the inn's sunroom; cordials in the lounge; library; concierge; turndown service; activities desk; room service (7am–10pm). *In room:* A/C, TV/VCR, dataport, hair dryer, iron, safe.

EXPENSIVE

Ansonborough Inn 🦀   This is one of the oddest hotels in the historic district. When they get past the not-very-promising exterior, most visitors really like the unusual configuration of rooms. Set close to the waterfront, the massive building, once a 1900 warehouse, has a lobby that features exposed timbers and a soaring atrium filled with plants. Despite the building's height, it only has three floors, which allows bedrooms to have ceilings of 14 to 16 feet and, in many cases, sleeping lofts. Bedrooms are outfitted with copies of 18th-century furniture and accessories, but the bathrooms are what you'd expect from a motel: molded-fiberglass shower stalls and imitation-marble countertops.

21 Hasell St., Charleston, SC 29401. © **800/522-2073** or 843/723-1655. Fax 843/577-6888. www.ansonboroughinn.com. E-mail: info@ansonboroughinn.com. 37 units. Mar–Nov $149–$259 double, off-season $109–$229 double Fri–Sat. Rates include continental breakfast. Children 11 and under stay free in parents' room. AE, DISC, MC, V. Free parking. **Amenities:** Breakfast; terrace with hot tub; dry cleaning. *In room:* A/C, TV, dataport, fridge, iron, safe.

Battery Carriage House Inn 🦀   In one of the largest antebellum neighborhoods of Charleston, this inn offers bedrooms in a carriage house behind the main building. In other words, the owners save the top living accommodation for themselves but have restored the bedrooms out back to a high standard. Recent renovations added four-poster beds and a colonial frill to the not-overly-large bedrooms. Don't stay here if you want an inn with lots of public space; that, you don't get. But you can enjoy the location, which is a short walk off the Battery—a seafront peninsula where you can easily imagine a flotilla of Yankee ships enforcing the Civil War blockades.

Unfortunately, if you call, you're likely to get only a recorded message until the owners are able to call you back. Despite the inaccessibility of the main house and the difficulty of reaching a staff member, this place provides comfortable and convenient lodging in a desirable neighborhood.

20 S. Battery, Charleston, SC 29401. ☏ 800/775-5575 or 843/727-3100. Fax 843/727-3130. www.batterycarriagehouse.com. E-mail: bch@mymailstation.com. 11 units. $99–$225 double. Rates include continental breakfast. AE, DISC, MC, V. Free parking. No children under 12. **Amenities:** Breakfast; afternoon tea; evening wine; concierge; twice-daily maid service with turndown. *In room:* A/C, TV.

Indigo Inn/Jasmine House ✮ These are a pair of hotels set across the street from each other, with the same owners and the same reception area in the Indigo Inn. Built as an indigo warehouse in the mid-19th century, and gutted and radically reconstructed, the Indigo Inn (the larger of the two) offers rooms with 18th-century decor and comfortable furnishings. Rooms in the Jasmine House, an 1843 Greek Revival mansion whose exterior is painted buttercup yellow, are much more individualized. Each room has a ceiling of about 14 feet, its own color scheme and theme, crown moldings, whirlpool tubs, and floral-patterned upholsteries. Parking is available only in the lot at the Indigo Inn.

1 Maiden Lane, Charleston, SC 29401. ☏ 800/845-7639 or 843/577-5900. Fax 843/577-0378. http://perl.webmillenia.net/IndigoInn/. E-mail: indigoinn@awod.com. 40 units (Indigo Inn), 10 units (Jasmine House). $159–$225 double in the Indigo Inn, $189–$250 double in the Jasmine House. Rates include continental breakfast. 10% discounts available in midwinter. AE, DISC, MC, V. Free parking. **Amenities:** Breakfast; concierge; some secretarial services. *In room:* A/C, TV.

John Rutledge House Inn ✮✮ Many of the meetings that culminated in the emergence of the United States as a nation were conducted in this fine 18th-century house, now the most prestigious inn in Charleston. The inn towers over its major rivals, such as the Planters Inn and the Ansonborough Inn, which are also excellent choices. The original builder, John Rutledge, was one of the signers of the Declaration of Independence; he later served as Chief Justice of the U.S. Supreme Court. The inn was built in 1763, with a third story added in the 1850s. Impeccably restored to its Federalist grandeur, it's enhanced with discreetly concealed electronic conveniences.

116 Broad St., Charleston, SC 29401. ✆ **800/476-9741** or 843/723-7999. Fax 843/720-2615. www.charminginns.com. E-mail: jrh@charminginns.com. 19 units. $165–$325 double; $290–$374 suite. Rates include continental breakfast. AE, DC, DISC, MC, V. Free parking. **Amenities:** Continental breakfast and tea and afternoon sherry served in upstairs sitting room; concierge, access to nearby health club; dry cleaning and laundry; massage; babysitting. *In room:* A/C, TV, dataport, fridge, hair dryer, iron.

Kings Courtyard Inn ✷

The tiny entry to this three-story 1853 inn in the historic district is deceiving, because it opens inside to a brick courtyard with a fountain. A fireplace warms the small lobby, which has a brass chandelier. Besides the main courtyard, two courts offer fine views from the breakfast room. The owners bought the building next door and incorporated 10 more rooms into the existing inn. Your room might be outfitted with a canopy bed, an Oriental rug over a hardwood floor, an armoire, or even a gas fireplace. Some rooms have refrigerators. Rates include evening chocolates and turn-down service. A whirlpool is on site.

198 King St., Charleston, SC 19401. ✆ **800/845-6119** or 843/723-7000. Fax 843/720-2608. www.charminginns.com. E-mail: kci@charminginns.com. 44 units. $150–$210 double. Rates include breakfast. Children 11 and under stay free in parents' room. Off-season 3-day packages available. AE, DC, DISC, MC, V. Parking $5. **Amenities:** Continental breakfast included in rate (a full breakfast is available at an additional charge); concierge; access to nearby health club; dry cleaning and laundry; massage; babysitting. *In room:* A/C, TV, dataport, fridge, hair dryer, iron.

Lodge Alley Inn ✷

This sprawling historic property extends from its entrance on the busiest commercial street of the Old Town to a quiet brick-floored courtyard in back. It was once a trio of 19th-century warehouses. Today, it evokes a miniature village in Louisiana, with a central square, a fountain, landscaped shrubs basking in the sunlight, and easy access to the hotel's Cajun restaurant, the French Quarter. Units include conventional and rather standard hotel rooms, suites, and duplex arrangements with sleeping lofts. Throughout, the decor is American country, with pine floors and lots of colonial accents. Some rooms have fireplaces, and most retain the massive timbers and brick walls of the original warehouses. The staff is usually polite and helpful, but because the hotel hosts many small conventions, they may be preoccupied with the demands of whatever group happens to be checking in or out.

195 E. Bay St., Charleston, SC 29401. ✆ **800/846-0009** or 843/722-1611. Fax 843/722-1611, ext. 7777. www.lodgealleyinn.com. 95 units. $149–$169 double; $175–$300 suite. Children 12 and under stay free in parents' room. AE, MC, V. Free valet parking. **Amenities:** Breakfast; room service; conference rooms; dry cleaning and laundry; babysitting; access to nearby health club. *In room:* A/C, TV, dataport, minibar, fridge, coffeemaker, hair dryer, iron.

Philip Porcher House ✿   Hailed by *Travel and Leisure* as one of the top B&Bs in the South, this beautifully restored 1770 Georgian home stands in the heart of the historic district. Built by a French Huguenot planter, Philip Porcher, the house was renovated in 1997. Handsome Georgian revival oak paneling was installed from the demolished executive offices of the Pennsylvania Railroad in Pittsburgh. The apartment was attractively furnished with period antiques and 18th-century engravings. The one rental unit on the ground floor consists of five rooms, and is rented to only one party (with two bedrooms, the apartment can accommodate up to four guests, ideal for families). Good books and music create a cozy environment. A comfortable sitting room has a working fireplace. One twin-bedded bedroom also has a fireplace. There is one bathroom with an elegant glass shower and double sinks. A screened gallery opens onto a wonderful secret walled garden.

19 Archdale St., Charleston 29401. ✆ **843/722-1801.** www.bbonline.com/ sc/porcher. E-mail: porcherhhome.com. 1-2 bedroom apt. $200 for two, $300 for four. Rates include continental breakfast. No credit cards. Free parking. *In room:* TV.

Two Meeting Street Inn ✿   Set in an enviable position near the Battery, this house was built in 1892 as a wedding gift from a prosperous father to his daughter. Inside, the proportions are as lavish and gracious as the Gilded Age could provide. Stained-glass windows, mementos, and paintings were either part of the original decorations or collected by the present owners, the Spell family. Most bedrooms contain four-poster beds, ceiling fans, and (in some cases) access to a network of balconies. A continental breakfast with home-baked breads and pastries is served.

2 Meeting St., Charleston, SC 29401. ✆ **843/723-7322.** 9 units. $165–$310 double. No credit cards. Rates include continental breakfast and afternoon tea. Free parking. No children under 12. **Amenities:** Concierge; nonsmoking rooms. *In room:* A/C, TV, hair dryer, iron, safe.

Vendue Inn ✿   This recently expanded, three-story inn manages to convey some of the personalized touches of a B&B. Its public areas—a series of narrow, labyrinthine spaces—are full of antiques and colonial accessories that evoke a cluttered, and slightly cramped, inn in Europe. Bedrooms do not necessarily follow the lobby's European model, however, and appear to be the result of decorative experiments by the owners. Room themes may be based on aspects of Florida, rococo Italy, or 18th-century Charleston. Marble floors and tabletops, wooden sleigh beds, and (in some rooms) wrought-iron canopy beds, while eclectically charming, might be inconsistent with your vision of colonial Charleston. Overflow guests are housed in a historic, brick-fronted annex across the cobblestone-covered street.

19 Vendue Range, Charleston, SC 29401. ✆ **800/845-7900** or 843/577-7970. Fax 843/722-8381. www.vendueinn.com. E-mail: vendueinnresv@aol.com. 65 units. $135–$189 double, $219–$295 suite. Rates include full Southern breakfast. AE, DC, DISC, MC, V. Valet parking $12 a day. **Amenities:** The Library at Vendue restaurant; The Roof Top Terrace restaurant, with a panoramic view of the harbor; concierge; meeting rooms; fitness center; laundry service; dry cleaning service; babysitting; full health club, massage, and bicycle rentals are nearby. *In room:* A/C, TV/VCR, dataport, hair dryer, iron, safe.

Westin Francis Marion Hotel 𝒜   A $14-million award-winning restoration has returned this historic hotel to its original elegance. Although the 12-story structure breaks from the standard Charleston decorative motif and has rooms furnished in traditional European style, it is not devoid of Charleston charm. Rooms feature a king, queen, or double bed, and recently renovated bathrooms are adorned with brass fixtures. The hotel's restaurant, Elliott's on the Square, features an extensive international and continental menu, serving dinner from 6:30 to 10pm and providing room service for hotel guests until 11pm. The hotel bar begins serving at 10am until 10pm.

387 King St., Charleston, SC 29403. ✆ **888/627-8510** or 843/722-0600. Fax 843/723-4633. www.weston.com. E-mail: westinfmsale@charleston.net. 226 units. $99–$205 double, $189–$319 suite. Children 11 and under stay free in parents' room. AE, CB, DC, DISC, MC, V. Parking $10–$14. **Amenities:** Restaurant; modem ports in each room; business services and meeting rooms; concierge; a fitness room; in-room massage. *In room:* A/C, TV.

MODERATE

Reliable motel accommodations are also available at the **Hampton Inn Historic District,** 345 Meeting St. (✆ **800/HAMPTON** or 843/426-7866), across from the visitor center.

Anchorage Inn 𝒜𝒜   Other than a heraldic shield out front, few ornaments mark this bulky structure, which was built in the 1840s as a cotton warehouse. The inn boasts the only decorative theme of its type in Charleston: a mock-Tudor interior with lots of dark paneling; references to Olde England; canopied beds with matching tapestries; pastoral or nautical engravings; leaded casement windows; and, in some places, half-timbering. Because bulky buildings are adjacent to the hotel on both sides, the architects designed all but a few rooms with views overlooking the lobby. (Light is indirectly filtered inside through the lobby's overhead skylights—a plus during Charleston's hot summers.) Each room's shape is different from that of its neighbors, and the expensive ones have bona fide windows overlooking the street outside.

26 Vendue Range, Charleston, SC 29401. © **800/421-2952** or 843/723-8300. Fax 843/723-9543. www.anchoragecharleston.com. E-mail: anchorage@islc.net. 19 units. $109–$149 double; $169–$210 suite. Rates include continental breakfast and afternoon tea. AE, MC, V. Parking $6. **Amenities:** Continental breakfast; afternoon tea, with sherry, wine, and cheese; concierge and tour desk. In room: A/C, TV.

Ashley Inn *⑀*   Partly because of its pink clapboards and the steep staircases that visitors must climb to reach the public areas, this imposing bed-and-breakfast inn might remind you of an antique house in Bermuda. Built in 1832 on a plot of land that sold at the time for a mere $419, it has a more appealing decor than the Cannonboro Inn, which belongs to the same Michigan-based owners. Breakfast and afternoon tea are served on a wide veranda overlooking a brick-paved driveway whose centerpiece is a formal fountain/goldfish pond evocative of Old Charleston. The public rooms, with their high ceilings and deep colors, are appealing. If you have lots of luggage, know in advance that negotiating this inn's steep and frequent stairs might pose something of a problem. None of the rooms contains a phone.

201 Ashley Ave., Charleston, SC 29403. © **800/581-6658** or 843/723-1848. Fax 843/723-8007. www.charleston-sc-inns.com. 7 units. $95–$139 double; $115–$175 queen; $135–$190 suite. Rates include full breakfast and afternoon tea. AE, MC, V. Free off-street parking. **Amenities:** Concierge; activities desk. In room: A/C, TV, iron.

Barksdale House Inn *⑀*   This is a neat, tidy, and well-proportioned Italianate building near the City Market, constructed as an inn in 1778 but altered and enlarged by the Victorians. Behind the inn, guests enjoy a flagstone-covered terrace where a fountain splashes. Bedrooms often contain four-poster beds and working fireplaces, and about half a dozen have whirlpool tubs. Throughout, the furnishings, wallpaper, and fabrics evoke the late 19th century. Sherry and tea are served on the back porch in the late afternoon.

27 George St., Charleston, SC 29401. © **888/577-4980** or 843/577-4800. Fax 843/ 853-0482. www.barksdalehouse.com. 14 units. Summer $135–$195 double. Off-season $110–$150. Rates include continental breakfast. AE, MC, V. Free parking. No children under 7. **Amenities:** Concierge; afternoon tea. In room: A/C, TV, dataport.

Cannonboro Inn   This buff-and-beige 1856 house was once the private home of a rice planter. The decor isn't as carefully coordinated or as relentlessly upscale as that of many of its competitors; throughout, it has a sense of folksy informality. Although there's virtually no land around this building, a wide veranda on the side creates a "sit-and-talk-a-while" mood. Each accommodation contains a canopy bed; formal, old-fashioned furniture; and cramped, somewhat dated bathrooms.

184 Ashley Ave., Charleston, SC 29403. ℭ **800/235-8039** or 843/723-8572. Fax 843/723-8007. www.charleston-sc-inns.com. E-mail: cannonboroinn@aol.com. 6 units. $95–$130 double; $115–$190 queen; $155–$210 suite. Rates include full breakfast and afternoon tea and sherry. AE, MC, V. Free parking. No children under 10. **Amenities:** Concierge; activities desk. *In room:* A/C, TV, iron.

Doubletree Guest Suites   A somber, five-story 1991 building adjacent to the historic City Market, the Doubletree (formerly the Hawthorne), offers suites instead of rooms, each outfitted with some type of kitchen facility, from a wet bar, refrigerator, and microwave oven to a fully stocked kitchenette with enough utensils to prepare a simple dinner. The accommodations here tend to receive heavy use, thanks to their appeal to families, tour groups, and business travelers. Breakfast is the only meal served. Amenities include a bar/lounge, a fitness center, a swimming pool, and a coin-operated laundry. Parking is available in the underground parking garage.

181 Church St., Charleston, SC 29401. ℭ **843/577-2644.** Fax 843/577-2697. www.doubletree.com. 181 units. $99–$189 1-bedroom suite; $200–$285 2-bedroom suite. Rates include buffet breakfast. AE, DC, DISC, MC, V. Parking $14. *In room:* A/C, TV.

1837 Bed & Breakfast   Built in 1837 by Nicholas Cobia, a cotton planter, this place was restored and decorated by two artists, and in 2001 underwent major renovations, with the addition of carved cornice moldings, French doors, and antique furnishings. It's called a "single house" because it's only a single room wide, which makes for some interesting room arrangements. Our favorite room is No. 2 in the Carriage House, which has authentic designs, exposed-brick walls, warm decor, a beamed ceiling, and three windows. All the rooms have refrigerators and separate entrances because of the layout, and all contain canopied four-poster rice beds. On one of the verandas, you can sit under whirling ceiling fans and enjoy your breakfast (sausage pie or eggs Benedict, and homemade breads) or afternoon tea. The parlor room has cypress wainscoting and a black-marble fireplace; the breakfast room is really part of the kitchen.

126 Wentworth St., Charleston, SC 29401. ℭ **877/723-1837** or 843/723-7166. Fax 843/722-7179. www.1837bb.com. 9 units. $69–$165 double. Rates include full breakfast. AE, MC, V. Free off-street parking. **Amenities:** Concierge. *In room:* A/C, TV, coffeemaker, fridge, hair dryer, iron.

Elliott House Inn   Historians have researched anecdotes about this place going back to the 1600s, but the core of the charming inn that you see today was built as a private home—probably for slaves—in 1861. You get a warm welcome from a very hip staff, and there's lots of colonial inspiration in the decor of the comfortable and carefully maintained rooms. But despite all the grace notes and the landscaping (the flowerbeds are touched up every 2 weeks), the place seems like a raffish, indoor/outdoor motel, which some guests find appealing. The rooms are arranged in a style that you might expect in Key West—off tiers of balconies surrounding a verdant open courtyard. Each room contains a four-poster bed (the one in No. 36 is especially nice) and provides a feeling of living in an upscale cottage. Avoid the units that have ground-level private outdoor terraces, however; they're cramped and claustrophobic, don't have attractive views, and tend to be plagued by mildew problems. Conversation often becomes free and easy beneath the city's largest wisteria arbor, near a bubbling whirlpool designed for as many as 12 occupants at a time.

78 Queen St. (between King and Meeting sts.), Charleston, SC 29401. (C) **800/ 729-1855** or 843/723-1855. Fax 843/722-1567. www.elliotthouseinn.com. 24 units. $135–$160 double, off-season $94–$105. Rates include continental breakfast. AE, DISC, MC, V. Parking $15. **Amenities:** Concierge; activities desk; lunch and dinner room service; bicycles; Jacuzzi. *In room:* A/C, TV, dataport, hair dryer, iron.

INEXPENSIVE

To avoid the high costs of the elegant B&Bs and deluxe inns of historic Charleston, try one of the chain motels such as **Days Inn,** 2998 W. Montague Ave., Charleston 29418 ((C) **843/747-4101;** fax: 843/566-0378), near the International Airport. Doubles range from $50 to $72, with an extra person housed for $6. Children under 12 stay free, and cribs are also free. **Lands Inn,** 2545 Savannah Hwy., Charleston 29414 ((C) **843-763-885;** fax 843/556-9536), is another bargain, with doubles costing from $69 to $79, and an $10 extra charged for each additional person. Children under 16 stay free. A final bargain is **Red Roof Inn,** 7480 Northwoods Blvd., Charleston 29406 ((C) **843/572-9100;** fax 843/572-0061), where doubles cost $44 to $57, and $7 charged for each additional person. Those 18 and under are housed free.

Best Western King Charles Inn   One block from the historic district's market area, this three-story hotel has rooms that are better than you might expect from a motel and are likely to be discounted

(*Kids*) **Family-Friendly Hotels**

Ansonborough Inn *(see p. 21)*   This is a good value for families that want to stay in one of the historic inns, as opposed to a cheap motel on the outskirts. Many of the high-ceilinged rooms in this converted warehouse have sleeping lofts.

Best Western King Charles Inn *(see p. 28)*   This is one of the best family values in Charleston. Children 17 and under stay free in their parents' room. The location is only a block from the historic district's market area, and there's a small pool.

Doubletree Guest Suites *(see p. 27)*   This is a good choice for families that want extra space and a place to prepare meals. Some suites are bilevel, giving families more privacy. The location is adjacent to the City Market.

Seagrass Inn *(see p. 30)*   Suites complete with kitchenettes make this inexpensive place an outstanding value for families. Two pools where you can cool off in the hot, humid weather add to the attraction.

off-season. Some rooms have balconies, but the views are limited. Although short on style, the King Charles is a good value and convenient to most everything. Breakfast is served in a colonial-inspired restaurant, and the hotel has a small pool and a helpful staff.

237 Meeting St. (between Wentworth and Society sts.), Charleston, SC 29401. (*C*) **800/528-1234** or 843/723-7451. Fax 843/723-2041. 91 units. $99–$199 double. Children 17 and under stay free in parents' room. AE, CB, DC, DISC, MC, V. Free parking. *In room:* A/C, TV.

King George IV Inn   This four-story 1790 Federal-style home in the heart of the historic district serves as an example of the way Charleston used to live. Named the Peter Freneau House, it was formerly the residence of a reporter and co-owner of the *Charleston City Gazette.* All rooms have wide-planked hardwood floors, plaster moldings, fireplaces, and 12-foot ceilings, and are furnished with antiques. Beds are either Victorian or four-poster double or queen-size. All guests are allowed access to the three levels of porches on the house. The location is convenient to many downtown

Charleston restaurants; tennis is a 5-minute drive, the beach is 15 minutes away, and some 35 golf courses are nearby. The continental breakfast consists of cereals, breads, muffins, and pastries.

32 George St., Charleston, SC 29401. ☎ **888/723-1667** or 843/723-9339. Fax 843/723-7749. www.kinggeorgeiv.com. E-mail: info@kinggeorgeiv.com. 10 units 2 with shared baths. $99–$175 double without bath. $125–$159 double. Rates include continental breakfast. AE, MC, V. Free parking. *In room:* A/C, TV.

Rutledge Victorian Guest House   This 19th-century structure is a sibling property of the King George IV Inn (described earlier in this section). The Italianate building is kept immaculate; rooms, as well as the inn, are furnished with Victorian antiques and have four-poster, rice, mahogany, or Italian rope beds in double, queen, and twin sizes. The location is just a short trek from many of Charleston's notable restaurants, and activities such as golf and tennis are just minutes away. Most rooms have working fireplaces and private baths. In addition, the Rutledge Victorian Guest House has accommodations at another nearby property, Number Six Ambrose Alley. Specify your room requests and accommodations when you make your reservation; doing so as far in advance as possible is highly recommended.

114 Rutledge Ave., Charleston, SC 29401. ☎ **888/722-7553** or 843/722-7551. Fax 843/727-0065. www.bbonline.com/sc/rutledge. E-mail: normlyn@prodigy.net. 10 units (8 with private bath). $89–$129 double without private bath, $109–$159 double with private bath. Rates include continental breakfast. MC, V. Free parking. *In room:* A/C, TV.

NORTH CHARLESTON
INEXPENSIVE

Seagrass Inn   There aren't many places in the Charleston area where families can rent suites, complete with kitchenettes, that start at $75 a night, but this is one of them. The double rooms, starting at $45 a night, also attract serious budgeteers, and there's more good news: 17 of the standard doubles also contain kitchenettes. Rooms, as you'd expect, are in the standard motel format that you've seen a thousand times, and suites are little more than a small living room and bedroom. A coin laundry and two swimming pools make this place especially popular with families traveling during the hot, humid months

2355 Aviation Ave., North Charleston, SC 29418. 11 miles NW of Historic District off Interstate 26. ☎ **800/845-1927** or 843/744-4900. Fax 843/745-0668. 242 rooms. $48 double, $78 suite. Rates include continental breakfast. AE, DC, DISC, MC, V. Free parking. **Amenities:** Pool; 24-hour diner (in spring 2002); coin laundry. *In room:* A/C, TV.

Ramada Inn   This major competitor of the Holiday Inns is hardly in the same class as the historic inns discussed earlier in this chapter, but it's kind to the frugal vacationer. An outpost for the weary interstate driver, the inn is convenient to the airport and major traffic arteries, and the hotel provides free transportation to and from the airport. Charleston's downtown mass transit system doesn't serve this area, however, so be warned that you'll have to depend on your car. Your buck gets more than you might expect at this well-run chain member. Although you don't get charm, you do get good maintenance and proper service, and a refrigerator and microwave are available upon request. An on-site restaurant serves three meals a day, and other choices (including a Red Lobster) are within walking distance. The hotel also offers a Ramada Live Lounge that features nightly entertainment ranging from country music to karaoke and even comedy specialties.

W. Montigue Ave., North Charleston, SC 29418. 8 miles NW of Charleston off Interstate 26. (✆) **800/272-6232** or 843/744-8281. Fax 843/744-6230. www. ramada.com. 155 units. Mar–Oct, $105 double; off-season, $85 double. $10 each additional person. AE, DC, DISC, MC, V. Free parking. *In room:* A/C, TV.

4 Where to Dine

Foodies from all over the Carolinas and as far away as Georgia flock to Charleston for some of the finest dining in the tri-state area. You get not only the refined cookery of the Low Country, but also an array of French and international specialties. Space does not permit us to preview all the outstanding restaurants of Charleston—much less the merely good ones.

VERY EXPENSIVE

Circa 1886 Restaurant ✿✿ LOW COUNTRY/FRENCH Situated in the carriage house of the Wentworth Mansion (see earlier in this chapter), this deluxe restaurant offers grand food and formal service. Begin by taking the invitation of the concierge for a view of Charleston from the cupola, where you can see all the bodies of water surrounding the city. Seating 50, two main rooms are beautifully set, the most idyllic place for a romantic dinner in Charleston. The chef prepares an updated version of Low Country cookery, giving it a light, contemporary touch but still retaining the flavors of the Old South. Menus are rotated seasonally to take advantage of the best and freshest produce. For a first course, try the likes of crab cake soufflé with mango coulis and sweet pepper sauce, or a Southern shrimp spring roll with peanut sauce. For the main course, opt for the lavender poached spiny lobster with artichokes or blackened mahi-mahi with a coconut rice pilaf.

Special attention is paid to the salad courses, as exemplified by a concoction of baby spinach, strawberries, wild mushrooms, and red onion, all flavored with a champagne-and-poppy-seed vinaigrette.

Desserts, ordered at the beginning of the meal, include a unique baked Carolina with orange and raspberry sorbets or pan-fried angel food cake with fresh berries and peach ice cream.

In the Wentworth Mansion, 149 Wentworth St. © **843/853-1886.** Reservations required. Main courses $18.50–$38.50. AE, DC, DISC, MC, V.

Louis's Restaurant and Bar *rr* MODERN/LOW COUNTRY Renowned Chef Louis Osteen opened this restaurant to rave reviews on March 1, 1998. After learning his craft in the kitchens of the French restaurants of Atlanta and in his own Low Country kitchen on Pawley's Island, Osteen brought his talents to the Charleston Place Hotel in 1989 and opened Louis's Charleston Grill, where he embraced the new culinary movement of American regionalism— with immediate success. His fame grew, and his desire to reach a larger audience gave birth to his current kitchen. The restaurant's decor is by Adam Tihany, known for his designs for New York's Le Cirque 2000. He turned the restaurant into a work of art, with a design that's both efficient and quietly graceful.

The menu changes frequently. But if you've ever dined at the Charleston Grill, you will recognize his signature dishes. Starters, such as McClellanville lump crabmeat with melted butter on avocado blini or Mediterranean mussels steamed in Belgian beer, will whet your appetite absolutely. Main courses range from grouper wrapped in pancetta with gingered carrots and parsnip broth to properly aged and meltingly tender black Angus strip steak with green-peppercorn-and-Calvados sauce. The desserts are best complemented by a glass of port. The wine list is vast—the largest in Charleston.

Louis's list of awards and recognitions reads almost like a resume. He was twice nominated by the James Beard Foundation as the American Express Chef Southeast.

200 Meeting St., at the corner of Pinckney Street, in the Bank of America Building. © **843/853-2550.** Reservations required. Main courses $16–$32. AE, DC, DISC, MC, V. Daily 5–10pm.

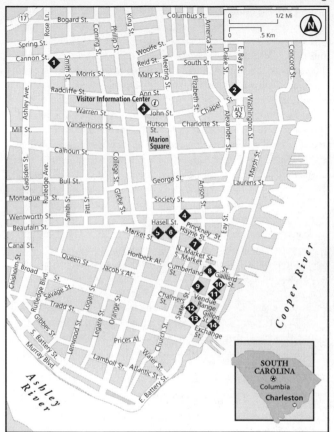

A.W. Shucks **12**

Anson **7**

The Boathouse of East Bay **2**

Carolina's **14**

Charleston Grill **13**

Circa 1886 Restaurant **16**

82 Queen **15**

High Cotton **8**

Hominy Grill **1**

Hyman's Seafood Company Restaurant **6**

Joe Pasta **3**

Louis's Restaurant and Bar **4**

Magnolias **9**

Peninsula Grill **5**

Robert's of Charleston **11**

S.N.O.B. (Slightly North of Broad) **10**

Robert's of Charleston 🦀🦀🦀 FRENCH   One of the most unusual restaurants in Charleston, and one of the best and most exclusive, this formal choice is a winner in cuisine, service, and ambience. Chef/owner Robert Dickson has brought a whole new dimension to dining in Charleston. His set menu, which is served in a long, narrow room that evokes an intimate dinner party, is the town's finest.

Guests peruse the menu while listening to music from a pianist. The waiter will explain each course on a menu that is seasonally adjusted. He'll also give you a preview of each wine that you'll be served. Don't be surprised if the chef himself suddenly bursts through the door from the kitchen in the back, singing *Oliver's* "Food, Glorious Food." Each dish we've ever sampled here has been a delight in flavor and texture, ranging from sea scallops mousse in a Maine lobster sauce as an appetizer, to very tender, rosy duck breast in a yellow pepper cream sauce. The garnishes served with the dishes—often ignored in most restaurants—are especially tasty here, including roasted red pepper or hot fried eggplant. Tossed in a homemade vinaigrette, salads are zesty with wild mixed greens and such vegetables as mushrooms and artichokes. For a main course, dig into a chateaubriand with a demi-glaze flavored with mushrooms from the woods, or perhaps steamed salmon. Desserts often include the best and richest chocolate cake in Charleston. It comes with vanilla sauce, strawberries, and almond praline, but perhaps that's gilding the lily.

182 East Bay St. ⓒ **843/577-7565.** Reservations essential. 7-course fixed-price menu including wine and coffee. $75 per person. One-seating Thurs–Sat 7:30pm. AE, DC, MC, V.

EXPENSIVE

Anson 🦀🦀🦀 LOW COUNTRY/MODERN AMERICAN   We think it's simply the best. Charlestonians know that they can spot the local society types here; newcomers recognize it as a hip, stylish venue with all the grace notes of a top-notch restaurant in New York or Chicago, but with reminders of Low Country charm. The setting is a century-old, brick-sided ice warehouse. The present owners have added New Orleans–style iron balconies, Corinthian pilasters salvaged from demolished colonial houses, and enough Victorian rococo for anyone's taste. A well-trained staff in long white aprons describes dishes that are inspired by traditions of the coastal Southeast. But this isn't exactly down-home cookery, as you'll see after sampling the fried cornmeal oysters with potato cakes; the lobster, corn, and black-bean quesadillas; the cashew-crusted grouper with champagne sauce; and a perfectly prepared rack of lamb in a crispy Dijon-flavored crust with mint sauce. Our favorite is the crispy flounder, which rival chefs have tried to duplicate but haven't equaled.

12 Anson St. ℭ 843/577-0551. Reservations recommended. Main courses $16.95–$26.95. AE, DC, DISC, MC, V. Sun–Thurs 5:30–11pm, Fri–Sat 5:30pm–midnight.

⟨ OUTSTANDING ⟩

Charleston Grill ✦✦✦ LOW COUNTRY/FRENCH Chef Bob Waggoner, from the Wild Boar in Nashville, has a devoted local following. This is the most ostentatiously formal and pleasing restaurant in Charleston, with superb service, grand food, an impeccably trained staff, and one of the city's best selections of wine. His French cuisine draws rave reviews, earning the restaurant the Mobil Four-Star rating—the only restaurant in South Carolina to have such a distinction. The decor makes absolutely no concessions to Southern folksiness, and the marble-floored, mahogany-sheathed dining room is one of the city's most luxurious. Menu items change with the seasons, and you will be pleasantly surprised by how well Low Country and French cuisine meld. Some absolutely delectable items include chilled summer carrot and sweet cantaloupe soup; Maine lobster tempura served over lemon grits with fried green tomatoes in a yellow tomato and tarragon butter; and, most delightful, McClellanville lump crabmeat cakes with roasted pistachio and a chive sauce. Not to be missed is red deer tenderloin over honey-roasted pears with almonds in a sweet cranberry and orange coulis. For something more down-home, try Okeechobee catfish with poached crayfish tails over succotash in a Chardonnay-and-thyme-flavored butter sauce.

In the Charleston Place Hotel, 224 King St. ℭ 843/577-4522. Reservations recommended. Main courses $17–$29. AE, DISC, DC, MC, V. Sun–Thurs 6–10pm, Fri–Sat 6–11pm.

⟨ GOOD – NOT GREAT ⟩

Peninsula Grill ✦✦ CONTINENTAL/INTERNATIONAL There's an old Southern saying about "country come to city." This is one case where "city has come to country." The Peninsula Grill, in the historic Planters Inn, has caused quite a stir in the gastronomic world—not just in Charleston, but also around the country. Quaint and quiet, the setting has a 19th-century charm unlike any other restaurant in Charleston. The menu changes frequently. You may start with James Island clams with wild-mushroom bruschetta or roasted-acorn-squash soup. Main courses run the gamut from the succulent chargrilled double pork chops with hoop cheddar grits to the to-die-for, pistachio-crumb-crusted sea bass. The kitchen does a marvelous job of bringing new cuisine to an old city without compromising the delicacies that have made dining in Charleston famous.

In the Planters Inn, 112 N. Market St. © **843/723-0700.** Reservations required. Main courses $18–$28. AE, DC, DISC, MC, V. Mon–Thurs 5:30–10pm, Fri–Sat 5:30–11pm.

MODERATE

The Boathouse on East Bay SEAFOOD   Briny delights await you at this bustling restaurant at the corner of Chapel and East Bay. It is a curious blend of family friendliness and two-fisted machismo, appealing to a wide range of denizens from Charleston plus visitors who are just discovering the place. The setting is in a turn-of-the-century warehouse where boats were once repaired. Massive antique timbers on the heavily trussed ceiling remain. On the northern perimeter of the historic core, the restaurant has a raw bar open daily from 4 to midnight. Shellfish platters are the chef's specialty, including the $69 "J Boat," which can be shared. On it is some of the city's best oysters, littleneck clams, smoked mussels, king crab legs, and fresh shrimp. Every night four different types of fish, ranging from mahi-mahi to black grouper, are grilled and served with a range of sauces, from mustard glaze to hoisin ginger.

Familiar Charleston specialties include shrimp and grits and crab cakes with green Tabasco sauce, the latter being one of our favorites. For those who don't want fish, a selection of pasta, beef, and chicken dishes are also served. For dessert, opt for the strawberry cobbler or Key lime pie.

549 E. Bay St. Reservations recommended. Main courses $12.95–$22.95. AE, MC, V. Sun–Thurs 5–10pm, Fri–Sat 5–11pm.

Carolina's AMERICAN   This restaurant is usually included on any local resident's short list of noteworthy local bistros. An antique warehouse has been transformed into a stylish, minimalist enclave of hip, where old-time dishes are prepared with uptown flair: sweet potato–encrusted flounder filet, loin of lamb with Carolina rose eggplant and sun-dried tomato chutney, the best crab cakes in town, and an almost excessively elaborate version of local grouper cooked in almond-and-black-sesame-seed crust and topped with crabmeat and lemon-butter sauce. As you dine, admire the antique French movie posters on the walls.

10 Exchange St. 🕐 **843/724-3800**. www.carolinasrest.com. Reservations recommended. Main courses $8–$32. AE, DISC, DC, MC, V. Mon–Thurs 5:30–11pm, Fri–Sun 5–11pm.

82 Queen 🐟 LOW COUNTRY   In its way, this is probably the most unusual compendium of real estate in Charleston: three 18th- and 19th-century houses clustered around an ancient magnolia tree, with outdoor tables arranged in its shade. Menu items filled with flavor and flair include an award-winning version of she-crab soup laced with sherry; grilled Carolina quail served over creamy grits with skillet gravy; down-home shrimp-and-chicken gumbo with andouille sausage, stewed tomatoes, and okra; and melt-in-the-mouth crab cakes with sweet-pepper-and-basil rémoulade sauce.

82 Queen St. 🕐 **843/723-7591**. www.82queen.com. Reservations recommended for dinner. Main courses $17–$23. AE, DC, MC, V. Lunch daily 11:30am–4pm. Dinner Sun–Thurs 6–10pm, Fri & Sat 5:30–10:30pm.

High Cotton SOUTHERN/STEAK   Established in 1999, this is a blockbuster of a restaurant, catering to an increasingly devoted clientele of locals who prefer its two-fisted drinks in an upscale macho decor, and a tasty cuisine that defines itself as a Southern-style steakhouse. It's also a good choice for nightlife because of its busy and cozy bar. If you decide to stick around for dinner, expect more than steaks. Dig into the buttermilk-fried oysters with arugula in a green goddess dressing, or order the terrine of foie gras. (How did that get on the menu?) Follow with such delights as medallions of venison with glazed carrots in a red wine and juniper sauce. Most diners go for one of the juicy steaks, which are tender and succulent, and served with sauces ranging from bourbon to béarnaise. Most dishes are moderate in price. You can also order items such as roasted squab with a potato and leek hash and a particularly lavish Charleston-style praline soufflé.

199 E. Bay St. 🕐 **843/724-3815**. Reservations recommended. Main courses $15–$34. AE, DC, MC, V. Sun–Fri 5:30–10pm, till 11pm on Fri & Sat. Bar opens at 4pm.

Magnolias SOUTHERN   Magnolias manages to elevate the regional, vernacular cuisine of the Deep South to a hip, postmodern art form that's suitable for big-city trendies, but is more likely to draw visiting tourists instead. The city's former Customs House has been revised into a sprawling network of interconnected spaces with heart-pine floors, faux-marble columns, and massive beams. Everybody's favorite lunch here is an open-face veal meatloaf sandwich—which, frankly, we find to be rather dull. But the soups and salads tend to be excellent; try the salad made with field greens, lemon-lingonberry vinaigrette, and crumbled bleu cheese. Down South dinners include everything from Carolina carpetbaggers beef filet with Parmesan-fried oysters, green beans, Madeira and béarnaise sauce, to chicken and dumplings with shiitake mushrooms.

185 E. Bay St. © **843/577-7771.** Reservations recommended. Main courses $14.50–$24.95. AE, DC, MC, V. Sun–Thurs 11:30am–10pm, Fri–Sat 11:30am–11pm.

S.N.O.B. (Slightly North of Broad) SOUTHERN   You'll find an exposed kitchen, a high ceiling crisscrossed with ventilation ducts, and vague references to the South of long ago—including a scattering of wrought iron—in this snazzily rehabbed warehouse. The place promotes itself as being Charleston's culinary maverick, priding itself on updated versions of the vittles that kept the South alive for 300 years, but frankly, the menu seems to be tame compared with the innovations being offered at many of its upscale, Southern-ethnic competitors. After you get past the hype, however, you might actually enjoy the place. Former diners include Timothy ("007") Dalton, Lee Majors, Sly Stallone, and superlawyer Alan Dershowitz. Main courses can be ordered in medium and large sizes—a fact appreciated by dieters. Flounder stuffed with deviled crab, grilled dolphin glazed with pesto on a bed of tomatoes, and grilled tenderloin of beef with green-peppercorn sauce are examples of this place's well-prepared—but not particularly Southern—menu. For dessert, make it the chocolate pecan torte. Together with sibling restaurants, Slightly Up the Creek and Elliott's on the Square, the restaurant has launched a private-label wine, dubbed MSK (for "Maverick Southern Kitchen").

192 E. Bay St. © **843/723-3424.** Reservations accepted only for parties of 6 or more. Main courses $10–$22. AE, DC, DISC, MC, V. Mon–Fri 11:30am–3pm and 5:30–11pm, Sat–Sun 5:30–11pm.

INEXPENSIVE

A.W. Shucks SEAFOOD   This is a hearty oyster bar, a sprawling, salty tribute to the pleasures of shellfish and the fishers who gather them. A short walk from the Public Market, in a solid, restored warehouse, the setting is one of rough timbers with a long bar where thousands of crustaceans have been cracked open and consumed, as well as a dining room. The menu highlights oysters and clams on the half-shell, tasty seafood chowders, deviled crab, shrimp Creole, and succulent oysters prepared in at least half a dozen ways. Chicken and beef dishes are also listed on the menu, but they're nothing special. A wide selection of international beers is sold. Absolutely no one cares how you dress; just dig in.

70 State St. ℂ **843/723-1151**. Lunch $5–$11. Main courses $13–$20. AE, DC, DISC, MC, V. Sun–Thurs 11am–10pm, Fri–Sat 11am–11pm.

Hominy Grill ⟨ LOW COUNTRY   Owned and operated by Chef Robert Stehling, Hominy Grill features simply and beautifully prepared dishes inspired by the kitchens of the Low Country. Since its opening, it has gained a devoted local following, who come here to feast on such specialties as barbecue chicken sandwich, avocado and wehani rice salad and grilled vegetables, okra and shrimp beignets, and—a brunch favorite—smothered or poached eggs on homemade biscuits with mushroom gravy. At night, try oven-fried chicken with spicy peach gravy (yes, that's right) or grilled breast of duck with eggplant and sautéed greens. Stehling claims that he likes to introduce people to new grains in the place of pasta or potatoes; many of his dishes, including salads, are prepared with grains such as barley and cracked wheat. The menu is well balanced between old- and new-cookery styles. Dropping in for breakfast? Go for the buttermilk biscuits, the meaty bacon, and the home-style fried apples. There's even liver pudding on the menu. A lunch of catfish stew with cornbread is a temptation on a cold, rainy day, and the banana bread is worth writing home about.

207 Rutledge Ave. ℂ **843/937-0930**. Fax 843/937-0931. www.hominygrill.com. Brunch from $10; lunch main courses $5–$9; dinner main courses $9–$18. MC, V. Breakfast Mon–Fri 7:30–11am; lunch Mon–Fri 11:30am–2:30pm; dinner Mon–Thurs 5:30–9:30pm, Fri & Sat 5:30–10pm; Sat–Sun brunch 9am–2:30pm.

Hyman's Seafood Company Restaurant ⟨ SEAFOOD Hyman's was established a century ago and honors old-fashioned traditions. The building sprawls over most of a city block in the heart of Charleston's business district. Inside are at least six dining rooms and a take-away deli loaded with salmon, lox, and smoked herring, all displayed in the style of the great kosher delis of New York City. One sit-down section is devoted to deli-style sandwiches, chicken soup, and salads; another, to a delectably messy choice of fish, shellfish, lobsters, and oysters. We can ignore the endorsement of old-time Sen. Strom Thurmond, but we take more seriously the praise of such big-time foodies as Barbra, Oprah, and Baryshnikov. Come early or late to avoid waiting in line.

(Kids Family-Friendly Restaurants

Magnolias *(see p. 37)*   Southern hospitality and charm keep this place buzzing day and night. Lunch is the best time for families and children. An array of soups, appetizers, salads, sandwiches, and pastas is available. But in-the-know local kids go easy on these items, saving room for homemade fare such as the warm cream-cheese brownie with white-chocolate ice cream and chocolate sauce.

Hominy Grill *(see p. 39)*   Locally loved, this grill has been a friendly, homelike family favorite since 1996. Fair prices, good food, and an inviting atmosphere lure visitors to sample an array of Southern specialties at breakfast, lunch, or dinner.

215 Meeting St. ✆ 843/723-6000. www.hymansseafood.com. Reservations not accepted. Lunch $5–$10; seafood dinners and platters $12–$20. AE, DISC, MC, V. Mon–Fri 11am–11pm, Sat–Sun 7am–11pm; restaurant closes at 10pm in winter and late fall.

Joe Pasta ITALIAN/PASTA   Favored by college students and budget-conscious locals, this is a clean, well-organized pasta joint evocative of an Italian trattoria with a full bar and a standard, limited, but still savory menu. Pasta can be ordered with at least four different degrees of doneness, ranging from al dente to mushy. Begin with soup or the house salad or perhaps one of the appetizers such as an antipasti platter or bruschetta—here, garlic bread topped with a tomato and fresh basil salad. Sandwiches range from meatball Parmesan to chicken. But pastas dominate the menu, and the sauces go from pesto to marinara. We're fond of the baked ziti with three cheeses. Finish off with an Italian ice or a piece of cheesecake.

428 King St. ✆ 843/965-5252. Reservations not needed. Sandwiches 95¢ each, all pastas $4.50. DISC, MC, V. Tues–Thurs 11:30am–11pm, Fri–Sat 11:30am–midnight.

5 Seeing the Sights

We always head for the **Battery** (officially, the White Point Gardens) to get into the feel of this city. It's right on the end of the peninsula, facing the Cooper River and the harbor. It has a landscaped park, shaded by palmettos and live oaks, with walkways

Charleston Sights

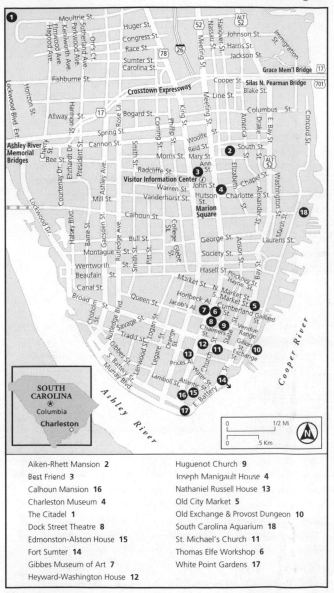

SOUTH
CAROLINA
✱
Columbia
○
Charleston

Aiken-Rhett Mansion **2**	Huguenot Church **9**
Best Friend **3**	Joseph Manigault House **4**
Calhoun Mansion **16**	Nathaniel Russell House **13**
Charleston Museum **4**	Old City Market **5**
The Citadel **1**	Old Exchange & Provost Dungeon **10**
Dock Street Theatre **8**	South Carolina Aquarium **18**
Edmonston-Alston House **15**	St. Michael's Church **11**
Fort Sumter **14**	Thomas Elfe Workshop **6**
Gibbes Museum of Art **7**	White Point Gardens **17**
Heyward-Washington House **12**	

lined with old monuments and other war relics. The view toward the harbor goes out to Fort Sumter. We like to walk along the seawall on East Battery and Murray Boulevard and slowly absorb the Charleston ambience.

Note that you can visit several of the attractions listed in this section by buying a Passport Ticket for $29. The ticket provides admission to Middleton Place, Drayton Hall, the Nathaniel Russell House, the Gibbes Museum, and the Edmondston-Alston House.

THE TOP ATTRACTIONS
A NATIONAL MONUMENT

Fort Sumter National Monument 🎯🎯🎯   It was here that the first shot of the Civil War was fired on April 12, 1861. Confederate forces launched a 34-hour bombardment of the fort. Union forces eventually surrendered, and the Rebels occupied federal ground that became a symbol of Southern resistance. This action, however, led to a declaration of war in Washington. Amazingly, Confederate troops held onto Sumter for nearly 4 years, although it was almost continually bombarded by the Yankees. When evacuation finally came, the fort was nothing but a heap of rubble.

Park rangers today are on hand to answer your questions, and you can explore gun emplacements and visit a small museum filled with artifacts related to the siege. A complete tour of the fort, conducted daily from 9am to 5pm, takes about 2 hours.

Though you can travel to the fort via your own boat, most people take the tour of the fort and harbor offered by **Fort Sumter Tours,** 205 King St., Suite 204 (𝄞 **843/722-1691**). You can board at either of two locations: Charleston's City Marina on Lockwood Boulevard or Mount Pleasant's Patriots Point, the site of the world's largest naval and maritime museum. Sailing times change every month or so, but from March to Labor Day, there generally are three sailings per day from each location, beginning at 9:30 or 10:45am. Winter sailings are more curtailed. Call for details. Each departure point offers ample parking, and the boats that carry you to Fort Sumter are sightseeing yachts built for the purpose; they're clean, safe, and equipped with modern conveniences.

In Charleston Harbor. 𝄞 **843/883-3123** or 843/722-1691. Admission: Fort, free; boat trip, $11 adults, $6 children 6–11 (children 5 and under free).

HISTORIC HOMES

Edmondston-Alston House 🎯🎯🎯   On High Battery, an elegant section of Charleston, this house (built in 1825 by Charles

Edmondston, a Charleston merchant and wharf owner) was one of the earliest constructed in the city in the late Federalist style. Edmondston sold it to Charles Alston, a Low Country rice planter, who modified it in Greek Revival style. The house has remained in the Alston family, which opens the first two floors to visitors. Inside are heirloom furnishings, silver, and paintings. It was here in 1861 that General Beauregard joined the Alston family to watch the bombardment of Fort Sumter. Gen. Robert E. Lee once found refuge here when his hotel uptown caught on fire.

21 East Battery. 𝒞 843/722-7171. Admission $7; included in Passport Ticket (see "Seeing the Sights," above). Guided tours Tues–Sat 10am–4:30pm, Sun–Mon 1:30–4:30pm.

Nathaniel Russell House 🐸🐸🐸 One of America's finest examples of Federal architecture, this 1808 house was completed by Nathaniel Russell, one of Charleston's richest merchants. It is celebrated architecturally for its "free-flying" staircase, spiraling unsupported for three floors. The staircase's elliptical shape is repeated throughout the house. The interiors are ornate with period furnishings, especially the elegant music room with its golden harp and neoclassical-style sofa.

51 Meeting St. 𝒞 843/724-8481. www.historiccharleston.org. Admission $7; included in Passport Ticket (see "Seeing the Sights," above). Guided tours Mon–Sat 10am–4:30pm, Sun and holidays 2–4:30pm.

Heyward-Washington House 🐸🐸🐸 In a district of Charleston called Cabbage Row, this 1772 house was built by Daniel Heyward, called "the rice king," and was the setting for Dubose Heyward's *Porgy.* It was also the home of Thomas Heyward, Jr., a signer of the Declaration of Independence. President George Washington bedded down here in 1791. Many of the fine period pieces in the house are the work of Thomas Elfe, one of America's most famous cabinetmakers. The restored 18th-century kitchen is the only historic kitchen in the city that is open to the public. It stands behind the main house, along with the servants' quarters and the garden.

87 Church St. (between Tradd and Elliott sts.). 𝒞 843/722-0354. Admission $8 adults, $4 children 3–12; combination ticket to the Charleston Museum and Joseph Manigault House, $18. Mon–Sat 10am–5pm, Sun 1–5pm. Tours leave every half hour until 4:30pm.

Calhoun Mansion 🐸🐸 This 1876 Victorian showplace is complete with period furnishings (including a few original pieces); porcelain-and-etched-glass gas chandeliers; ornate plastering; and cherry, oak, and walnut woodwork. The ballroom's 45-foot-high ceiling has a skylight. A freestanding spiral staircase is one of the remarkable features of this house. Among the tales of its many vicissitudes is the rescue of the once-deteriorating house by the U.S. Navy, which painted it battleship-gray inside and out.

16 Meeting St. (between Battery and Lamboll sts.). ℂ 843/722-8205. Admission $15 adults, $7 children 6–10. Wed–Sun 10am–4pm. Closed holidays.

Joseph Manigault House ℛ This 1803 Adams-style residence, a National Historic Landmark, was a wealthy rice planter's home. The house features a curving central staircase and an outstanding collection of Charlestonian, American, English, and French period furnishings. It's located diagonally across from the visitor center.

350 Meeting St. (at John St.). ℂ 843/722-2996. Admission $8 adults, $4 children 3–12; combination ticket to the Heyward-Washington House and Charleston Museum, $18. Mon–Sat 10am–5pm, Sun 1–5pm.

NEARBY PLANTATIONS

Middleton Place ℛℛℛ This was the home of Henry Middleton, president of the First Continental Congress, whose son, Arthur, was a signer of the Declaration of Independence. Today, this National Historic Landmark includes America's oldest landscaped gardens, the Middleton Place House, and the Plantation Stableyards.

The gardens, begun in 1741, reflect the elegant symmetry of European gardens of that period. Ornamental lakes, terraces, and plantings of camellias, azaleas, magnolias, and crape myrtle accent the grand design.

The Middleton Place House itself was built in 1755, but in 1865, all but the south flank was ransacked and burned by Union troops. The house was restored in the 1870s as a family residence and today houses collections of fine silver, furniture, rare first editions by Catesby and Audubon, and portraits by Benjamin West and Thomas Sully. In the stable yards, craftspeople demonstrate life on a plantation of yesteryear. There are also horses, mules, hogs, cows, sheep, and goats.

A plantation lunch is served at the Middleton Place Restaurant, which is a replica of an original rice mill. *American Way* magazine cited this restaurant as being one of the top 10 representing American cuisine at its best. Specialties include she-crab soup, Hoppin' John and ham biscuits, okra gumbo, Sea Island shrimp, and corn pudding. Service is daily from 11am to 3pm. Dinner is served daily 5 to 9pm, and is likely to include panned quail with ham, sea scallops, or broiled oysters. For dinner reservations, call ℂ **843/556-6020.**

Ashley River Rd. ℂ **843/556-6020.** Admission $18 adults, $15 children 6–12, free children 5 and under. Tour of House, additional $15, children 6–12 $7. Gardens and stable yards daily 9am–5pm; house Mon 1:30–4:30pm, Tues–Sat 10:30am–4:30pm. Take U.S. 17 west to S.C. 61 (Ashley River Rd.) 14 miles northwest of Charleston.

Magnolia Plantation 🦌🦌🦌 Ten generations of the Drayton family have lived here continuously since the 1670s. They haven't had much luck keeping a roof over their heads; the first mansion burned just after the Revolution, and the second was set afire by General Sherman. But you can't call the replacement modern. A simple, pre-Revolutionary house was barged down from Summerville and set on the basement foundations of its unfortunate predecessors.

The house has been filled with museum-quality Early American furniture, appraised to exceed $500,000 in value. An art gallery has been added to the house as well.

The flowery gardens of camellias and azaleas—among the most beautiful in America—reach their peak bloom in March and April but are colorful year-round. You can tour the house, the gardens (including an herb garden, horticultural maze, topiary garden, and biblical garden), a petting zoo, and a waterfowl refuge, or walk or bike through wildlife trails.

Other sights include an antebellum cabin that was restored and furnished, a plantation rice barge on display beside the Ashley River, and a Nature Train that carries guests on a 45-minute ride around the plantation's perimeter.

Low Country wildlife is visible in marsh, woodland, and swamp settings. The **Audubon Swamp Garden,** also on the grounds, is an independently operated 60-acre cypress swamp that offers a close look at other wildlife, such as egrets, alligators, wood ducks, otters, turtles, and herons.

S.C. 61. ℂ **800/367-3517** or 843/571-1266. Admission to garden and grounds, $11 adults, $10 seniors, $9 children 13–19, $5 children 6–12. Tour of plantation house is an additional $6 for ages 6 and up; children under 6 not allowed to tour the house. Admission to Audubon Swamp Garden, $5 adults and seniors, $4 children 13–19, $3 children 6–12. Magnolia Plantation and Audubon Swamp Gardens, summer daily 8am–5:30pm, winter daily 9am–5pm.

Drayton Hall 🦌🦌 This is one of the oldest surviving plantations, built in 1738 and owned by the Drayton family until 1974. Framed by majestic live oaks, the Georgian-Palladian house is a property of the National Trust for Historic Preservation. Its hand-carved wood-work and plasterwork represent New World craftsmanship at its finest. Because such modern elements as electricity, plumbing, and central heating have never put in an appearance, the house is much as it was in its early years; in fact, it is displayed unfurnished.

Old Ashley River Rd. (S.C. 61). ✆ **843/766-0188.** Admission $8 adults, $6 children 12–18; $4 children 6–11; included in Passport Ticket (see "Seeing the Sights," above). Mar–Oct, daily 10am–4pm, with tours on the hour; Nov–Feb, daily 9:30am–3pm. Closed Thanksgiving Day and Dec 25. Take U.S. 17 S. to S.C. 61; it's 9 miles northwest of Charleston.

Boone Hall Plantation 🎟   This unique plantation is approached by a famous **Avenue of Oaks** 🎟🎟🎟, huge old moss-draped trees planted in 1743 by Capt. Thomas Boone. The first floor of the plantation house is elegantly furnished and open to the public. Outbuildings include the circular smokehouse and slave cabins constructed of bricks made on the plantation. A large grove of pecan trees lies behind the house. Note that Boone Hall is not an original structure, but a replica; diehard history purists may be dis-appointed in the plantation house, but the grounds are definitely worth seeing.

Long Point Rd. (U.S. 17/701), Mt. Pleasant. ✆ **843/884-4371.** Admission $12.50 adults, $10 seniors 55 and over, $8 children 6–12. Apr–Labor Day, Mon–Sat 8:30am–6:30pm, Sun 1–5pm; day after Labor Day–Mar, Mon–Sat 9am–5pm, Sun 1–4pm. Take U.S. 17/701 9 miles north of Charleston.

SPECTACULAR GARDENS

See also the listing for Magnolia Plantation in "Nearby Plantations," earlier in this chapter.

Cypress Gardens 🎟🎟   This 163-acre swamp garden was used as a freshwater reserve for Dean Hall, a huge Cooper River rice plan-tation, and was given to the city in 1963. Today, the giant cypress trees draped with Spanish moss provide an unforgettable setting for flat-bottom boats that glide among their knobby roots. Footpaths in the garden wind through a profusion of azaleas, camellias, daffodils, and other colorful blooms. Visitors share the swamp with alligators, pileated woodpeckers, wood ducks, otters, barred owls, and other abundant species. The gardens are worth a visit at any time of year, but they're at their most colorful in March and April. Closed: Thanksgiving; December 22 to February 21.

U.S. 52, Moncks Corner. ✆ **843/553-0515.** $7 adults, $6 seniors, $2 children 6–16. Daily 9am–5pm. Closed Jan. Take U.S. 52 some 24 miles north of Charleston.

MUSEUMS

Charleston Museum 🦀🦀 The Charleston Museum, founded in 1773, is the first and oldest museum in America. The collections preserve and interpret the social and natural history of Charleston and the South Carolina coastal region. The full-scale replica of the famed Confederate submarine *Hunley* standing outside the museum is one of the most-photographed subjects in the city. The museum also exhibits the largest silver collection in Charleston; early crafts; historic relics; and the state's only "Discover Me" room, which has hands-on exhibits for children.

360 Meeting St. ℂ **843/722-2996**; www.charlestonmuseum.com. Admission $8 adults, $4 children 3–12; combination ticket to the Joseph Manigault House and Heyward-Washington House, $18. Mon–Sat 9am–5pm, Sun 1–5pm.

Gibbes Museum of Art 🦀 Established in 1905 by the Carolina Art Association, the Gibbes Museum contains an intriguing collection of prints and drawings from the 18th century to the present. On display are landscapes, genre scenes, panoramic views of Charleston harbor, and portraits of South Carolinians (see *Thomas Middleton* by Benjamin West, *Charles Izard Manigault* by Thomas Sully, or *John C. Calhoun* by Rembrandt Peale). The museum's collection of some 400 miniature portraits ranks as one of the most comprehensive in the country.

The Wallace Exhibit has 10 rooms, 8 replicated from historic American buildings and 2 from classic French styles. Styles range from the plain dining room of a sea captain's house on Martha's Vineyard to the elegant drawing room of Charleston's historic Nathaniel Russell House (see "Historic Homes," above).

135 Meeting St. ℂ **843/722-2706**. www.gibbes.com. Admission $7 adults, $6 seniors and students and military, $3 children 6–18, children under 6 are free; included in Passport Ticket (see "Seeing the Sights," above). Tues–Sat 10am–5pm, Sun 1–5pm. Closed Mondays and holidays.

MORE ATTRACTIONS

Charles Towne Landing 🦀🦀🦀 This 663-acre park is located on the site of the first 1670 settlement. Underground exhibits show the colony's history, and the park features a re-creation of a small village, a full-scale replica of a 17th-century trading ship, and a tram tour for $1 (or you can rent a bike). Because trade was such an important part of colonial life, a full-scale reproduction of the 17th-century trading vessel *Adventure* is an excellent addition to the site. After touring the ship, you can step into the Settler's Life Area and view a 17th-century crop garden where rice, indigo, and cotton were grown. There's no flashy theme-park atmosphere here: What you see as you walk under huge old oaks, past freshwater lagoons, and through the Animal Forest (with the same species that lived here in 1670) is what those early settlers saw.

1500 Old Towne Rd. (S.C. 171, between U.S. 17 and I-126). ℂ **843/852-4200.** Admission $5 adults, $2.50 seniors and children 6–14, free for those with disabilities. Daily 8:30am–6pm.

Charleston Tea Plantation ℱ   This plantation is the only one in America that actually grows tea, sold as American Classic tea. The plantation has been growing tea since 1799, when a French botanist brought the first tea plants to Charleston. Today, the plantation uses a state-of-the-art harvesting machine (designed on-site) that you can see on the free tours offered during the harvest season. Private tours, costing $5 per person, are available for groups of 20 or more; you must make an appointment. Note that inclement weather cancels any tour. Be sure to buy some tea while you're here; you won't find anything fresher in the stores.

6617 Maybank Hwy. (15 miles S of Charleston on Wadmalaw Island). ℂ **843/ 559-0383.** Free admission. May–Oct, first Sat of each month 10am–1pm (tours on the half-hour).

Citadel ℱ   The all-male (at that time) Citadel was established in 1842 as an arsenal and a refuge for whites in the event of a slave uprising. In 1922, it moved to its present location.

The school received worldwide notoriety in 1995 during the failed attempt of Shannon Faulkner to join the ranks of the cadets. After winning a legal battle to be admitted, she dropped out, citing continual harassment as the cause. Faulkner's ordeal drew fiercely divided opinions. As best-selling author Pat Conroy, a Faulkner supporter, said, "They made sure that everyone in America saw that that college hates women." Conroy's novel *The Lords of Discipline* is based on his 4 years at the school. Since then, four more women have been admitted, two of whom have remained.

The campus of this military college features buildings of Moorish design, with crenellated battlements and sentry towers. It is especially interesting to visit on Friday, when the college is in session and the public is invited to a precision-drill parade on the quadrangle at 3:45pm. For a history of the Citadel, stop at the **Citadel Memorial Archives Museum** (ℂ **843/953-6846**).

Moultrie St. and Elmwood Ave. ℂ **843/953-3294.** Free admission. Daily 24 hours for drive-through visits; museum, Sun–Fri 2–5pm, Sat noon–5pm. Closed religious and school holidays.

Old Exchange & Provost Dungeon ✪   This is a stop that many tourists overlook, but it's one of the three most important colonial buildings in the United States because of its role as a prison during the American Revolution. In 1873, the building became City Hall. You'll find a large collection of antique chairs, supplied by the local Daughters of the American Revolution, each of whom brought a chair here from home in 1921.

122 E. Bay St. ⓒ **843/727-2165.** Admission $6 adults, $5.50 seniors, $3.50 children 7–12. Daily 9am–5pm. Closed Thanksgiving Day, Dec 23–25.

Fort Moultrie   Only a palmetto-log fortification at the time of the American Revolution, the half-completed fort was attacked by a British fleet in 1776. Col. William Moultrie's troops repelled the invasion in one of the first decisive American victories of the Revolution. The fort was subsequently enlarged into a five-sided structure with earth-and-timber walls 17 feet high. The British didn't do it in, but an 1804 hurricane ripped it apart. By the War of 1812, it was back and ready for action.

Osceola, the fabled leader of the Seminoles in Florida, was incarcerated at the fort and eventually died here. During the 1830s, Edgar Allen Poe served as a soldier at the fort. He set his famous short story "The Gold Bug" on Sullivan's Island. The fort also played roles in the Civil War, the Mexican War, the Spanish-American War, and even in the two World Wars, but by 1947, it had retired from action.

1214 Middle St., on Sullivan's Island. ⓒ **843/883-3123.** Admission $4 adults, $2 child under 15 and seniors over 62. Federal Recreation Passports honored. Daily 9am–5pm. Closed Christmas Day. Take S.C. 103 from Mt. Pleasant to Sullivan's Island.

Southern Carolina Aquarium ✪   Visitors can explore Southern aquatic life in an attraction filled with thousands of enchanting creatures and plants in amazing habitats, from five major regions of the Appalachian Watershed. Jutting out into the Charleston Harbor for 2,000 feet, the focal point at this brand-new attraction, which opened in 2000, is a 93,000-square-foot aquarium featuring a two-story Great Ocean Tank Exhibition. Contained within are some 800 animals, including deadly sharks but also sea turtles and stingrays. Every afternoon at 4pm the aquarium offers a dolphin program, where bottle-nosed dolphins can be viewed from an open-air terrace. One of the most offbeat exhibits replicates a blackwater swamp, with atmospheric fog, a spongy floor, and twinkling lights.

100 Aquarium Wharf. ℂ 843/720-1990. Admission $14 adults, $12 students 13–17, $7 youth 4–12. Children under 3 admitted free. July–Aug daily 9am–7pm, Sept–Oct and May–June daily 10am–5pm; off season daily 10am–5pm.

ESPECIALLY FOR KIDS

For more than 300 years, Charleston has been the home of pirates, patriots, and presidents. Your child can see firsthand the **Great Hall at the Old Exchange,** where President Washington danced; the **Provost Dungeons,** where South Carolina patriots spent their last days; and touch the last remaining structural evidence of the **Charleston Seawall.** Children will take special delight in **Charles Towne Landing** and **Middleton Place.** At **Fort Sumter,** they can see where the Civil War began. Children will also enjoy **Magnolia Plantation,** with its Audubon Swamp Garden.

Kids and Navy vets will also love the aircraft carrier **USS *Yorktown,*** at Patriots Point, 2 miles east of the Cooper River Bridge. Its World War II, Korean, and Vietnam exploits are documented in exhibits, and general naval history is illustrated through models of ships, planes, and weapons. You can wander through the bridge wheelhouse, flight and hangar decks, chapel, and sick bay, and view the film *The Fighting Lady,* which depicts life aboard the carrier. Also at Patriots Point are the nuclear ship *Savannah,* the world's first nuclear-powered merchant ship; the World War II destroyer *Laffey;* the World War II submarine *Clamagore;* and the cutter *Ingham.* Patriots Point is open daily from 9am to 6pm April to October, until 5pm November to March. Admission is $11 for adults, $10 for seniors over 62 and military personnel in uniform, $5 for kids 6 to 11. Adjacent is the fine 18-hole public Patriots Point Golf Course. For further information, call ℂ 843/884-2727.

Another kid-pleaser, **Best Friend,** adjacent to the visitor center on Ann Street (ℂ 843/973-7269), combines a museum and an antique train. The train features a full-size replica of the 1830 locomotive that was the first steam engine in the United States used for regularly scheduled passenger service. The train was constructed from the original plans in 1928 and donated to Charleston in 1993. Hours are Monday to Saturday from 9am to 5pm and on Sunday from 1 to 5pm; admission is free.

6 Organized Tours

BY HORSE & CARRIAGE   The **Charleston Carriage Co.,** 96 N. Market St. (ℂ 843/577-0042), offers narrated horse-drawn-carriage tours through the historic district daily from 9am to dusk.

There's free shuttle service from the visitor center and downtown hotels. The cost is $17 for adults, $15 for seniors and military personnel, and $8 for children 6 to 12.

BY MULE TEAM **Palmetto Carriage Tours,** 40 N. Market St., at Guignard Street (© **843/723-8145**), uses mule teams instead of the usual horse and carriage for its guided tours of Old Charleston. Tours originate at the Big Red Bar behind the Rainbow Market. The cost is $17 for adults, $15 for senior citizens, and $6 for children 6 to 11. Daily 9am to 5pm.

BY BOAT **Fort Sumter Tours,** 205 Kings St., Suite 204 (© **843/ 722-1691**), offers a **Harbor and Fort Sumter Tour** by boat, departing daily from the City Marina and from the Patriots Point Maritime Museum. This is the only tour to stop at Fort Sumter, target of the opening shots of the Civil War. Adults $11, children 6–12 $6. The operator also has an interesting **Charleston Harbor Tour,** with daily departures from Patriots Point. The 2-hour cruise passes the Battery, Charleston Port, Castle Pinckney, Drum Island, Fort Sumter, and the aircraft carrier *Yorktown,* and sails under the Cooper River Bridge and on to other sights. $10.50 for adults, children $5.50.

WALKING TOURS One of the best offbeat walking tours of Charleston is the **Charleston Tea Party Walking Tour** (© **843/ 577-5896**). It lasts 2 hours and costs $13 for adults or $6 for children up to age 12. Departing year-round Monday to Saturday at 9:30am (returning at 2pm), tours originate at the Kings Courtyard Inn, 198 Kings St. The tour goes into a lot of nooks and crannies of Charleston, including secret courtyards and gardens. Finally, you get that promised tea.

The embattled city of Charleston during one of the worst phases in its history comes alive again on the **Civil War Walking Tour,** conducted daily at 9am by a guide well versed in the lore of "The War of Northern Aggression." You can stroll down cobblestone streets and listen to firsthand accounts and anecdotes of Charleston during its years of siege by Union troops. Tours depart March to December, Wednesday to Sunday at 9am from the Mills House Hotel Courtyard at 115 Meeting St. Adults pay $15, and children 12 and under go free. Call Jack Thomson at © **843/722-7033** for more information; reservations are appreciated.

Tours of Charleston's 18th-century **architecture** in the original walled city begin at 10am, and tours of 19th-century architecture along Meeting Street and the Battery begin at 2pm. Departures are from in front of the Meeting Street Inn, 173 Meeting St. Tours last 2 hours and are given daily. The cost is $15 (free for children 12 and under). For reservations, call ✆ **843/893-2327.**

7 Beaches & Outdoor Pursuits

BEACHES   Three great beaches are within a 25-minute drive of the center of Charleston.

In the West Islands, **Folly Beach,** which had degenerated into a tawdry Coney Island–type amusement park, is making a comeback following a multimillion-dollar cleanup, but it remains the least-pristine beach in the area. The best bathroom amenities are located here, however. At the western end of the island is the **Folly Beach County Park,** with bathrooms, parking, and shelter from the rain. To get here, take U.S. 17 East to S.C. 171 South to Folly Beach.

In the East Cooper area, both the **Isle of Palms** and **Sullivan's Island** offer miles of public beaches, mostly bordered by beachfront homes. Windsurfing and jet skiing are popular here. Take U.S. 17 East to S.C. 703 (Ben Sawyer Boulevard). South Carolina 703 continues through Sullivan's Island to the Isle of Palms.

Kiawah Island has the area's most pristine beach—far preferable to Folly Beach, to our tastes—and draws a more up-market crowd. The best beachfront is at **Beachwalker County Park,** on the southern end of the island. Get there before noon on weekends; the limited parking is usually gone by then. Canoe rentals are available for use on the Kiawah River, and the park offers not only a boardwalk but also bathrooms, showers, and a changing area. Take U.S. 17 E to S.C. 171 South (Folly Beach Road), turn right onto S.C. 700 SW (Maybank Highway), to Bohicket Road, which turns into Betsy Kerrigan Parkway. Where Betsy Kerrigan Parkway dead-ends, turn left on Kiawah Parkway, which takes you to the island.

For details on the major resorts on Kiawah Island and the Isle of Palms, see chapter 3, "Coastal Adventures: Side Trips from Charleston."

BIKING   Charleston is basically flat and relatively free of traffic, except on its main arteries at rush hour. Therefore, biking is a popular local pastime and relatively safe. Many of the city parks have biking trails. Your best bet for rentals is **The Bicycle Shoppe,** 280 Meeting St. (✆ **843/722-8168**), which rents bikes for $4 per hour or $15 for a full day. A credit-card imprint is required as a deposit.

BOATING A true Charlestonian is as much at home on the sea as on land. Sailing local waters is a popular family pastime. One of the best places for rentals is **Wild Dunes Yacht Harbor,** Isle of Palms (© **843/886-5100**), where 16-foot boats, big enough for four people, rent for $165 for 4 hours, plus fuel. A larger pontoon boat, big enough for 10, goes for $260 for 4 hours, plus fuel.

DIVING Several outfitters provide rentals and ocean charters, as well as instruction for neophytes. **Aqua Ventures,** 426 W. Coleman Blvd., Mt. Pleasant (© **843/884-1500**), offers diving trips off the local shoreline at a cost of $60 to $80 per person. You can rent both diving and snorkeling equipment. Diving equipment costs $32 or $14 for a regulator. It's open Monday to Saturday from 10am to 6pm.

The Wet Shop, 5121 Rivers Ave. (© **843/744-5641**), rents scuba equipment for $45 a day, including two tanks, a regulator, wetsuit, diving knife, and weight belt. It's open July and August, Monday to Saturday from 10am to 6pm.

FISHING Freshwater fishing charters are available year-round along the Low Country's numerous creeks and inlets. The water-ways are filled with flounder, trout, spot-tail, and channel bass. Some of the best striped-bass fishing available in America can be found at nearby Lake Moultrie.

Offshore-fishing charters for reef fishing (where you'll find fish such as cobia, black sea bass, and king mackerel) and for the Gulf Stream (where you fish for sailfish, marlin, wahoo, dolphin, and tuna) are also available. Both types of charters can be arranged at the previously recommended **Wild Dunes Yacht Harbor,** Isle of Palms (© **843/886-5100**). A fishing craft holding up to six people rents for $725 for 6 hours, including everything but food and drink. Reservations must be made 24 hours in advance.

Folly Beach Fishing Pier at Folly Beach is a wood pier, 25 feet wide, that extends 1,045 feet into the Atlantic Ocean. Facilities include restrooms, a tackle shop, and a restaurant. It's handicapped accessible.

Those who'd like a true Low Country experience might even want to try crabbing or shrimping.

GOLF Charleston is said to be the home of golf in America. Charlestonians have been playing the game since the 1700s, when the first golf clubs arrived from Scotland. With 17 public and pri-vate courses in the city, there's a golf game waiting for every buff.

Wild Dunes Resort, Isle of Palms (© **803/886-6000**), offers two championship golf courses designed by Tom Fazio. **The Links** is a 6,722-yard, par-72 layout that takes the player through marshlands, over or into huge sand dunes, through a wooded alley, and into a pair of oceanfront finishing holes once called "the greatest east of Pebble Beach, California." The course opened in 1980 and has been ranked among the 100 greatest courses in the United States by *Golf Digest* and among the top 100 in the world by *Golf Magazine*. *Golf Digest* has also ranked the Links as the 13th-greatest resort course in America. **The Harbor Course** offers 6,402 yards of Low Country marsh and Intracoastal Waterway views. This par-70 layout is considered to be target golf, challenging players with two holes that play from one island to another across Morgan Creek. Greens fees at these courses can range from $42 to $100, depending on the season. Clubs can be rented at either course for $25 for 18 holes, and professional instruction costs $45 for a 45-minute session. Both courses are open daily from 7am to 6pm year-round.

Your best bet, if you'd like to play at any of the other Charleston-area golf courses, is to contact **Charleston Golf Partners** (© **800/774-4444** or 843/847-9770, Monday to Friday from 10am to 6pm). The company represents 15 golf courses, offering packages that range from $89 to $110 per person March to August. Off-season packages range from $69 to $99 per person. Prices include greens fees on one course, a hotel room based on double occupancy, and taxes. Travel professionals here will customize your vacation with golf-course selections and tee times; they can also arrange rental cars and airfares.

HIKING   The most interesting hiking trails begin around Buck Hall in **Francis Marion National Forest** (© **843/887-3257**), located some 40 miles north of the center of Charleston via U.S. 52. The site consists of 250,000 acres of swamps, with towering oaks and pines. Also in the national forest, **McClellanville,** reached by U.S. 17/701 north from Charleston, has 15 camping sites (cost: $10 per night), plus a boat ramp and fishing. Other hiking trails are at **Edisto Beach State Park,** State Cabin Road, on Edisto Island (© **843/869-2156**).

HORSEBACK RIDING   Our pick is **Seabrook Island Resort,** 1002 Landfall Way, Seabrook Island (© **843/768-1000**), although reservations for these guided rides are required 3 or 4 days in advance. The resort has an equestrian center and offers both trail rides and beach rides. The beach ride (for advanced riders only) leaves at 8am daily and costs $70 per person; the trail ride (also for advanced riders) leaves at 10:30am daily, going for $60 per person. For beginners, the "Walking Scenic" ride is offered; it lasts 1 hour and costs $50.

PARASAILING   Island Water Sports, South Beach Marina (© **843/671-7007**), allows you to soar up to 700 feet. The cost ranges from $45 to $55, depending on the length of line used. It's open April to October only, daily from 11am to 8pm.

TENNIS   Charlestonians have been playing tennis since the early 1800s. The **Charleston Tennis Center,** Farmfield Avenue (west of Charleston on U.S. 17), is your best bet, with 15 well-maintained outdoor courts lighted for night play. The cost is only $2.50 per person per hour of court time. The center is open Monday to Thursday from 8:30am to 10pm, on Friday from 8:30am to 7pm, on Saturday from 9am to 6pm, and on Sunday from 10am to 6pm.

At the **Shadowmoss Plantation Golf & Country Club,** 20 Dunvegan Dr. (© **843/556-8251**), nonmembers can play free (as space allows) daily from 7am to 7pm. Call ahead for court times.

WINDSURFING   The temperate waters and wide open spaces make the Low Country a favorite of windsurfers. Windsurfing can be arranged through **McKevlin's Surf Shop,** 1101 Ocean Blvd., Isle of Palms (© **843/886-8912**), which rents surfboards for $5 per hour. It's open in summer daily from 10am to 6pm; off-season, call for hours, which are subject to change.

8 Shopping

King Street is lined with many special shops and boutiques. The **Shops at Charleston Place,** 130 Market St., is an upscale complex of top designer-clothing shops (Gucci, Jaeger, Ralph Lauren, and so on), and the lively **State Street Market,** just down from the City Market, is another cluster of shops and restaurants.

ART

African American Art Gallery   With some 2,900 square feet of exhibition space, this is the largest African-American art gallery in the South. The original pieces change every 2 months. On permanent display are the works of prominent artists including Dr. Leo Twiggs and historical artist Joe Pinckney. Monday to Saturday: 10am to 6pm. 43 John St. © **843/722-8224.**

Lowcountry Artists In a former book bindery, this gallery is operated by eight local artists, who work in oil, watercolor, drawings, collage, woodcuts, and other media. Monday to Saturday: 10am to 5pm, Sunday noon to 5pm. 87 Hasell St. ℭ 843/577-9295.

Waterfront Gallery Facing Waterfront Park, this gallery is the premier choice for the work of South Carolina artists. The works of 21 local artists are presented, with original works beginning at $95. For sale are pieces ranging from sculpture to oils. Monday to Thursday 11am to 6pm, Friday to Saturday 11am to 10pm. 215 E. Bay St. (across from Custom House). ℭ 843/722-1155.

Wells Gallery Artists from the Low Country and all over the Southeast are on display at this Charleston gallery. Specializing in Low Country landscapes, the gallery offers works by two of South Carolina's most respected artists: Betty Anglain Smith and Mickey Williams. Prices range from $300 to $12,000. Monday to Saturday 10am to 6pm. 103 Broad St. ℭ 843/853-3233.

ANTIQUES

George C. Birlant and Co If you're in the market for 18th- and 19th-century English antique furnishings, this is the right place. This Charleston staple prides itself on its Charleston Battery Bench, which is seen (and sat upon) throughout the Battery. The heavy iron sides are cast from the original 1880 mold, and the slats are authentic South Carolina cypress. It's as close to the original as you can get. Monday to Saturday 9am to 5:30pm. 191 King St. ℭ 843/722-3842.

Livingston Antiques For nearly a quarter of a century, discriminating antiques hunters have patronized the showroom of this dealer. Both authentic antiques and fool-the-eye reproductions are sold. If you're interested, the staff will direct you to the shop's 30,000-square-foot warehouse on West Ashley. Monday to Friday 9am to 6pm, Saturday 10am to 4pm. 163 King St. ℭ 843/723-9697.

BOOKS

Atlantic Books Amelia and Gene Woolf offer thousands of good used books at moderate prices, along with a collection of rare books. The store's specialties are books on South Carolina and the Civil War. It also has a goodly collection of the works of Southern authors, along with modern first editions and books on Americana, children's literature, and nautical subjects. Monday to Saturday 10am to 6pm, Sunday 1 to 6pm. 310 King St. ℭ 843/723-4751.

CIVIL WAR ARTIFACTS

Sumter Military Antiques & Museum Relics from that "War of Northern Aggression" are sold here. You'll find a collection of authentic artifacts that range from firearms and bullets to Confederate uniforms and artillery shells and bullets. There are some interesting prints, along with a collection of books on the Civil War. Monday to Saturday 10am to 6pm. 54 Broad St. ℂ 843/577-7766.

CRAFTS & GIFTS

Charleston Crafts This is a permanent showcase for Low Country craft artists who work in a variety of media, including metal, glass, paper, clay, wood, and fiber. Handmade jewelry is also sold, along with basketry, leather, traditional crafts, and even home-made soaps. Monday to Saturday 10am to 6pm. 38 Queen St. ℂ 843/723-2938.

Clown's Bazaar Store owner Deanna Wagoner's heart is as big as her smile. Her store is indeed one of a kind—the city's only tax-exempt, self-help crafts organization. Originally, it was in Katmandu, Nepal, founded to help Third World families help themselves. Economic and political circumstances forced the store's relocation to Charleston, but the objective of helping Third World families hasn't changed. The store features handmade carvings, silks, brasses, and pewter from exotic locales such as Africa, Nepal, India, Bangladesh, and the Philippines, as well as wooden toys and books, including some in Gullah, a lost language that is still spoken in some areas of the city. Oh, and if you're looking for clown dolls, Deanna has those, too. Daily 11am to 5pm. 56 Broad St. ℂ 843/723-9769.

Wired & Fired This shop is a combination crafts shop and cafe established in the late 1990s. You enter what looks like an artist's studio in disarray, the walls containing shelves filled with unglazed ceramics. Clients buy the unglazed ceramics and apply the decorations themselves. Unglazed ceramics cost from $5 to $30 per object, plus a $3 firing fee. You are also charged $8 for time spent in the studio. Surprisingly, this is also one the most popular spots for a young man to take his girlfriend for the evening. Sunday 1 to 9pm, Monday 11am to 9pm, Tuesday to Thursday 11am to 10pm, Friday to Saturday 11am to midnight. 159 E. Bay St. ℂ 843/579-0999.

FASHION

Ben Silver One of the finer men's clothiers in Charleston, this is the best place to get yourself dressed like a member of the city's finest society. The store specializes in blazers and buttons; it has a collection of more than 600 blazer-button designs that are unique in the city. The store features house names and designs only, so don't go looking for Ralph Lauren here. Monday to Saturday 9am to 6pm. 149 King St. ✆ **843/577-4556.**

Nancy's   On the main street, Nancy's specializes in clothing for the woman who wants to be both active and stylish. Complete outfits in linen, silk, and cotton are sold, along with such accessories as belts and jewelry. Nancy's aims for a "total look." Monday to Saturday 10am to 5:30pm, Sunday 1 to 5pm. 342 King St. ✆ **843/ 722-1272.**

FURNISHINGS

Historic Charleston Reproductions   It's rare that a store with so much to offer could be not-for-profit, but that's the case here. All items are approved by the Historic Charleston Foundation, and all proceeds benefit the restoration of Charleston's historic projects.

Licensed-replica products range from furniture to jewelry. The pride of the store is its home-furnishings collection by Baker Furniture, an esteemed company based in Michigan. What makes this collection unusual is the fact that the pieces are adaptations of real Charleston antiques, made of mahogany, a rich dark wood with an authentic feel that can only be found here.

If one of Charleston's iron designs around town has caught your eye, there's a chance that you'll find a replica of it in the form of jewelry. A collection of china from Mottahedeh is also featured. Monday to Saturday 10am to 5pm.

The store operates shops in several historic houses, and for slightly more than basic souvenirs, see its **Francis Edmunds Center Museum Shop** at 108 Meeting St. (✆ **843/724-8484**; open Monday to Saturday 10am to 5pm, Sunday 2 to 5pm). 105 Broad St. ✆ **843/723-8292.**

HAMMOCKS

The Original Pawleys Island Rope Hammock   Looking for a backyard retreat after you return home? This shop may give you some ideas. Handmade quality and durability are the lure, because these hammocks have been made in the same way and in the same location for more than 100 years. Their creator, riverboat Capt. Joshua Ward, thought that the grass mattresses in his shop were too hot, not to mention quite uncomfortable. Because necessity is the mother of invention, he hand-wove the first Original Pawleys Island

Rope Hammock. You can choose between cotton and polyester ropes for your personal order. Monday to Friday 9:30am to 6pm, Sunday noon to 5pm. Hwy. 17, Pawleys Island. (C) 843/237-9122.

JEWELRY

Croghan's Jewel Box   You'll find gift ideas for any situation, from baby showers to weddings. Estate jewelry and some contemporary pieces are featured. This store also sets diamonds for rings and pendants, and can even secure the diamond for you, with the price depending on the type of stone and grade that you choose. Monday to Saturday 9:30am to 5:30pm. 308 King St. (C) 843/723-3594.

Dazzles   One-of-a-kind jewelry is sold here, along with the finest collection of handmade 14-karat-gold slide bracelets in town. Some of the jewelry is of heirloom quality. The staff will also help you create jewelry of your own design, including a choice of stones. Daily 10am to 7pm. Charleston Place, 226 King St. (C) 843/722-5951.

Geiss & Sons Jewelers   Jewelry here is custom-designed by Old World–trained craftspeople. This is a direct offshoot of a store opened by the Geiss family in Brazil in 1919. It's an official watch dealer for names such as Rolex, Bertolucci, and Raymond Weil. Repair jobs are given special attention. Monday to Saturday 10am to 5:30pm. 116 E. Bay St. (C) 843/577-4497.

JOGGLING BOARDS

Old Charleston Joggling Board Co.   Since the early 1830s, joggling boards have been a Charleston tradition. These boards are the creation of Mrs. Benjamin Kinloch Huger, a native who sought a mild form of exercise for her rheumatism. Mrs. Huger's Scottish cousins sent her a model of a joggling board, suggesting that she sit and gently bounce on the board. The fame of the device soon spread, and the board soon turned up in gardens, patios, and porches throughout the Charleston area. After World War II, joggling boards became rare because of the scarcity of timber and the high cost of labor, but the tradition was revived in 1970. The company also produces a joggle bench, a duplicate of the joggling board but only 10 feet long (as opposed to the original 16 feet) and 20 inches from the ground. Monday to Friday 8am to 5pm. 652 King St. (C) 843/723-4331.

PERFUME

Scents of Charleston   Favorite fragrances are found here, and prices (for the most part) are relatively reasonable. The shop evokes a perfumery in Europe. Scents creates its own exclusive brands, and also features classic and popular fragrances. Monday to Friday 10am to 9pm, Saturday to Sunday 9am to 5pm. 92 N. Market St. © 843/853-8837.

SMOKESHOP

The Smoking Lamp   This is Charleston's oldest smokeshop, with the most complete array of tobacco products in the city. You'll find an assortment of pipes, tobacco, cigars, even walking canes and other paraphernalia. Monday to Saturday 10am to 10pm, Sunday 11am to 6pm. 189 E. Bay St. © 843/577-7339.

9 Charleston After Dark

THE PERFORMING ARTS

Charleston's major cultural venue is the **Dock Street Theater,** 133 Church St. (© **843/965-4032**), a 463-seat theater. The original was built in 1736 but burned down in the early 19th century, and the Planters Hotel (not related to the Planters Inn) was constructed around its ruins. In 1936, the theater was rebuilt in a new location. It's the home of the **Charleston State Company,** a local not-for-profit theater group whose season runs from mid-September to May. Dock Street hosts various companies throughout the year, with performances ranging from Shakespeare to *My Fair Lady.* It's most active during the annual Spoleto Festival USA ℛ in May and June. The box office is open Monday to Thursday from noon to 5pm, on Friday and Saturday from 10am to 8pm, and on Sunday from 10am to 3pm.

The **Robert Ivey Ballet,** 1910 Savannah Hwy. (© **843/556-1343**), offers both classical and contemporary dance, as well as children's ballet programs. The group performs at various venues throughout the Charleston area, with general-admission prices of $18 for adults and $13 for children.

Charleston Ballet Theatre, 477 King St. (© 843/723-7334), is one of the South's best professional ballet companies. The season begins in late October and continues into April. Admission $15.

Charleston Symphony Orchestra, 14 George St. (© 843/723-7528), performs throughout the state, but its main venues are the Gaillard Auditorium and Charleston Southern University. The season runs from September to May.

THE CLUB & MUSIC SCENE

Cumberland's   If your musical tastes run from Delta blues to rock to reggae, this is the place for you. The dominant age group at this bar depends on the act playing. You will find that the generation gap isn't strong here, with college students toasting glasses with midlifers. Greasy chicken wings and lots of suds make this place ever popular. Music is the common bond. Daily 11am to 2am. 26 Cumberland St. © **843/577-9469.** Cover $3–$6.

Henry's   One of the best places for jazz in Charleston, this club features a live band on Friday and Saturday. Otherwise, you get taped top-40 music for listening and dancing. If you're a single man or woman with a roving eye, this is one of the hottest pick-up bars in town. It attracts mainly an over-30 crowd. Happy hour, with drink discounts and free appetizers, is Monday to Friday from 4 to 7pm. On Friday and Saturday evenings, the club hosts a Comedy Zone, with two shows nightly (8:30pm and 10:30pm). 54 N. Market St. © **843/723-4363** (© **843/853-8669** for Comedy Zone). Cover $12 for Comedy Show; no cover Sun–Thurs.

Music Farm   This club is self-described as being "Charleston's premier music venue." It covers nearly every taste in music, from country to rock. You're as likely to hear funkster George Clinton as you are country legend George Jones. The club hosts local and regional bands, as well as national acts. Music is present anywhere from 2 to 6 nights a week from 9am to 2am. Call **843/853-FARM** for schedules and information. 32 Ann St. © **843/722-8904.** Cover $2–$25.

Tommy Condon's Irish Pub   Located in a restored warehouse in the City Market area, this Irish pub and family restaurant is full of Old Ireland memorabilia. The bartender turns out a leprechaun punch, a glass of real Irish ale, and most definitely Irish coffee. The menu offers Irish food, along with Low Country specials such as shrimp and grits or jambalaya. Happy hour, with reduced drink prices, is Monday to Friday from 5 to 7pm. Live Irish entertainment is presented Wednesday to Sunday from 8:30pm until closing. Pub hours are Sunday to Thursday 11:30am to 10pm, Friday to Saturday 11am to 11pm. 160 Church St. © **843/577-3818.** No cover.

THE BAR SCENE

First Shot Bar   Our preferred watering hole is this old standby, where we've seen such visiting celebs as Gerald Ford and Elizabeth

Taylor (not together, of course) over the years. The bar is one of the most elegant in Charleston, a comfortable and smooth venue for a drink. If you get hungry, the kitchen will whip you up some shrimp and grits. In the Mills House Hotel, 115 Meeting St. (843/577-2400. No cover.

The Griffon   A lot of Scotch and beer is consumed at this popular Irish pub. A full array of home-cooked specials from the old country is served as well, including such pub-grub favorites as steak pies, bangers and mash (English sausage and mashed potatoes), and the inevitable fish and chips. Happy hour is Monday to Friday from 4 to 7pm. 18 Vendue Range. (843/723-1700. No cover.

Habana Club   With the ambience of a private club, this second-floor house from 1870 is where Ernest Hemingway would head if he were in Charleston today. Relax in one of three Gilded Age salons, each evocative of the Reconstruction era of the Old South. The house specializes in exotic cigars and martinis, and serves appetizers, desserts, fruit and cheese plates, and even some miniature beef Wellingtons. When filming *The Patriot,* Mel Gibson made Habana his second home in the city. You pass through a well-stocked tobacco store downstairs to reach the club. 177 Meeting St. (843/853-5900.

Jack's Tavern   Set in what was built in the 19th century as a warehouse, this neighborhood bar is lined with hand-made bricks and capped with heavy timbers. It receives a wide medley of drinkers, everyone from college students to local dockyard workers, as well as a scattering of travelers from out of town. Appetizers and burgers are the only food served, but at least a dozen beers are on tap. Live music begins at 9:30pm Wednesday to Saturday. The tavern is open Tuesday to Sunday 4pm to 2am. 213 E. Bay St. (843/720-7788.

Mike Calder's Pub   Mike Calder's place is a local favorite, with 15 imported beers on tap from England, Scotland, and Ireland. The bartender makes a mean Bloody Mary. 288 King St. (843/577-0123. No cover.

Vicery's Bar & Grill   This is one of the most popular gathering places in Charleston for the younger crowd, especially students. It's also a good dining choice, with an international menu that includes jerk chicken and gazpacho. But the real secrets of the place's success are its 16-ounce frosted mug of beer for $1 and the convivial atmosphere. 15 Beaufain. (843/577-5300. No cover.

MICROBREWERIES

For some, an evening in a microbrewery is the way to go in Charleston. Our favorites include **Southend Brewery & Smokehouse,** 161 East Bay St. (© **843-853-4677**), which specializes in wood-fired pizzas, freshly made salads, and barbecue. Of course, all this is washed down with a variety of original microbrews. You might also try **Zebo,** 275 King St. (© **843/577-7600**), a brewpub featuring a menu of wood-fired pizza, pasta, and appetizers along with a salad bar. Naturally, the home brew accompanies meals except at the Sunday brunch at 10:30am. This microbrewery rises three stories at the corner of Wentworth Street.

GAY & LESBIAN BARS

The Arcade   Set in the heart of historic Charleston, on the premises of what was once a 1930s movie theater, this is the largest and most high-energy dance bar in Charleston. Catering with equal ease to gays and lesbians, it features two to four bars (depending on the night of the week). The atmosphere ranges from quiet and conversational to danceaholic and manic. 5 Liberty St. © **843/722-5656.** Cover $3–$5.

Déjà Vu II   Some people say this is the coziest and warmest "ladies' bar" in the Southeast. Rita Taylor, your host, has transformed what used to be a supper club into a cozy enclave with two bars, weekend live entertainment (usually by "all-girl bands"), and a clientele that's almost exclusively gay and 75% lesbian. The ambience is unpretentious and charming, and definitely does not exclude sympathetic patrons of any ilk. 4634 Prulley Ave, N. Charleston. © **843/ 554-5959.** Cover $3–$5.

Dudley's   It's the coziest, clubbiest, and—in its low-key way— most welcoming gay bar in Charleston. Some regulars compare it with a gay version of "Cheers" because of its wood paneling and bricks, and its amused and bemused sense of blasé permissiveness. Most of the chatting occurs on the street level, where an advance call from nonmembers is considered to be necessary to guarantee admittance. Upstairs is a game room with pool tables and very few places to sit. The cover is charged as a means of ensuring status as a private club. 346 King St. © **843/723-2784.** Cover $1 after 8pm.

Patrick's Pub & Grill   If you like your men in leather, chances are you'll find Mr. Right here. A gay pub and grill, right outside Charleston, this is a late-night venue for some of the hottest men in

Charleston. Levis take second place to leather. 1377 Ashley River Rd. (Hwy. 61) ℰ 843/571-3435.

LATE-NIGHT BITES

Kaminsky's Most Excellent Café   Following a night of jazz or blues, this is a good spot to rest your feet and order just the power boost you need to make it through the rest of the evening. The handsome bar offers a wide selection of wines and is ideal for people-watching. Visitors who like New York's SoHo will feel at home here. The desserts are sinful, especially the Italian cream cake and mountain chocolate cake. Daily noon to 1am. 78 N. Market St. ℰ 843/853-8270.

3

Coastal Adventures: Side Trips from Charleston

From historic small towns to the intriguing landscapes of South Carolina's barrier islands, Charleston is surrounded by many fascinating places to explore. You can see the following destinations as quick day trips, but we've recommended a few lodging and restaurant choices in case you decide to linger.

For specifics on many of the area's outdoor activities, see "Beaches & Outdoor Pursuits," in chapter 2.

1 The Isle of Palms

A residential community bordered by the Atlantic Ocean and lying 10 miles north of Charleston, this island, with its salt marshes and wildlife, has been turned into a vacation retreat, but one that is more downscale than Kiawah Island. The attractions of Charleston are close at hand, but the Isle of Palms is also self-contained, with shops, dining, an array of accommodations, and two championship golf courses.

Charlestonians have been flocking to the island for holidays since 1898. The first hotel opened here in 1911. Seven miles of wide, white sandy beach are the island's main attraction, and sailing and windsurfing are popular. The more adventurous go crabbing and shrimping in the creeks.

GETTING THERE I-26 intersects with I-526 heading directly to the island via the Isle of Palms Connector (S.C. 517).

WHERE TO STAY & DINE

Wild Dunes Resort ✸✸ A bit livelier than Kiawah Island, its major competitor, this complex is set on landscaped ground on the north shore. The 1,600-acre resort has not only two widely acclaimed golf courses, but also an array of other outdoor attractions. Many families settle in here for a long stay, almost never venturing into Charleston. Guests are housed in condos and a series of cottages and villas. Many accommodations have only one bed-room, but others have as many as six. Villas and cottages are built along the shore, close to golf and tennis. You can also enjoy surf-casting, watersports, a racquet club, a yacht harbor on the Intracoastal Waterway, nature trails, and bicycling. Children's pro-grams are available. Furnishings are tasteful and resortlike, with kitchens, washers and dryers, and spacious bathrooms with dressing areas. Some of the best units have screened-in balconies. Edgar's Restaurant serves standard American cuisine and regional specialties.

Isle of Palms (P.O. Box 20575), Charleston, SC 29413. ℭ **800/845-8880** or 843/886-6000. Fax 843/886-2916. www.wilddunes.com. 312 units. $281–$550 villa or cottage. Golf packages available. AE, MC, V. Free parking. **Amenities:** Edgar's Restaurant; lounge (open until 2am); 2½ mile private beach; two outstanding golf courses; 19 hard-surface tennis courts; 20 pools. *In room:* A/C, TV.

2 Kiawah Island

This eco-sensitive private residential and resort community sprawls across 10,000 acres 21 miles south of Charleston. Named for the Kiawah Indians who inhabited the islands in the 17th century, it today consists of two resort villages: East Beach and West Beach. The community fronts a lovely 10-mile stretch of Atlantic beach; magnolias, live oaks, pine forests, and acres of marsh characterize the island.

Kiawah boasts many challenging golf courses, including one designed by Jack Nicklaus at Turtle Point that *Golf Digest* has rated among the top 10 courses in South Carolina. Golf architect Pete Dye designed a 2½ mile oceanfront course to host the 1991 PGA Ryder Cup March. *Tennis* magazine rates Kiawah as one of the nation's top tennis resorts, with its 28 hard-surface or Har-Tru clay courts. Anglers are also attracted to the island, especially in spring and fall.

GETTING THERE   To get here from Charleston, take S.C. 17 South to S.C. 700 West (Maybank Highway) to Bohicket Road. From there, follow the signs to Kiawah.

WHERE TO STAY & DINE

Kiawah Island Resort ⨁   A self-contained community, this complex opened in 1976 at West Beach village. Since then, East Beach village has joined the community. Regular hotel-style rooms are available in four buildings, opening onto the lagoon or the Atlantic. Rooms have one king or two double beds, along with private balconies and combination baths. Villas, with up to four bedrooms, are casually furnished and have complete kitchens and such amenities as washers and dryers.

Kiawah Island (P.O. Box 12357), Charleston, SC 29412. ℭ 800/654-2924 or 843/768-2122. Fax 843/768-9386. www.kiawahislandresort.com. E-mail: reservation@kiawahresort.com. 650 units. $139–$259 double; $139–$1,000 townhouse or villa. AE, DC, DISC, MC, V. **Amenities:** Several dining options include the Jasmine Porch and Veranda and Indigo House. Diners have tables facing the lagoon at the Park Cafe. Low Country and international dishes are featured. *In room:* A/C, TV.

3 Edisto Island

Isolated, and offering a kind of melancholy beauty, Edisto lies some 45 miles south of Charleston. By the late 18th century, Sea Island cotton made the islanders wealthy, and some plantations from that era still stand.

Today, the island attracts families from Charleston and the Low Country to its white sandy beaches. Watersports include shrimping, surf-casting, deep-sea fishing, and sailing.

GETTING THERE   Take U.S. 17 west for 21 miles; then head south along Highway 174 the rest of the way.

HITTING THE BEACH   **Edisto Beach State Park,** State Cabin Road, sprawls across 1,255 acres, opening onto 2 miles of beach. There's also a signposted nature trail. Enjoy a picnic lunch under one of the shelters. The park has 75 campsites with full hookups and 28 with no hookups. Campsites cost $20 per night (the price is the same for RV hookups). Five cabins are also available for rent, ranging from $62 to $67 daily. There are two restaurants within walking distance of the campsite, plus a general store nearby.

WHERE TO STAY

Fairfield Ocean Ridge ℛ   At the south end of Edisto Beach, this 300-acre resort is a favorite summer rendezvous for Charleston families. Birders flock to the area, as do shellers, and there is plenty of good fishing, along with summer picnics. It's an old-fashioned America-by-the-sea. Golf, jet skiing, parasailing, and tennis are among the other recreational activities. A timeshare resort, Fairfield rents villas and condos ranging from a one-bedroom villa up to a two-bedroom duplex villa with sleeping lofts. Each villa, complete with kitchen, is individually furnished according to the tastes of its owner. Most rooms have VCRs, and fax service is available at the rental office.

King Cotton Rd., Edisto Island, SC 29438. ℂ 800/845-8500 or 843/869-2561. www.fairfieldvacations.com. 40 units. $350 1-bedroom villa; $265 2-bedroom villa; $475 2-bedroom deluxe villa. AE, DC, DISC, MC, V. **Amenities:** Restaurant; free continental breakfast Mon only. *In room:* A/C, TV, minibar.

WHERE TO DINE

The Old Post Office ℛ SOUTHERN   This is the most prominent building that you're likely to see as you drive through the forests and fields across Edisto Island. About 5 miles from the beach, the restaurant was once a combination post office and general store, as its weathered clapboards and old-time architecture imply. Partners David Gressette and Philip Bardin, who transformed the premises in 1988, prepare a worthy compendium of Low Country cuisine and serve it in copious portions. Try Island corn and crabmeat chowder, Orangeburg onion sausage with black bean sauce, scallops and grits with mousseline sauce, fried quail with duck-stock gravy, and "fussed-over" pork chops with hickory-smoked tomato sauce and mousseline.

Hwy. 174 at Store Creek. ℂ 843/869-2339. Main courses $17–$22. MC, V. Mon–Sat 6–10pm.

Sunset Grille SEAFOOD   This is the sibling restaurant to The Old Post Office just recommended, and it is a family favorite. It opens onto Big Bay Creek overlooking the Intracoastal Waterway. The fresh fish and locally caught shellfish are delivered to the restaurant dock daily, and you can request it broiled, grilled, or fried. The lunch and dinner menus have variety, and the freshest of ingredients are used. The brunch on Sunday is the island's best. At lunch an array of fresh salads (including one made with local oysters) is served along with burgers, chicken grills, and a selection of the best-stuffed sandwiches on Edisto. You can also order a big bowl of South Carolina she-crab soup. The menu at night is more elaborate, with a selection of appetizers ranging from a fish stew in a robust tomato and fish stock to fried alligator served with honey mustard. New York strip appears as a main course, as do the delicious Edisto crab cakes. "Bell Boil" is a local favorite, fresh shrimp boiled in seasoned stock and served hot.

3701 Docksite Rd. at the Edisto Marina. ℂ 843/869-1010. Reservations not needed. Main courses $5–$18. MC, V. Mon–Sat 11am–10pm.

4 Beaufort

Some 30 miles north of Hilton Head Island, Beaufort (Low Country pronunciation *Bew*-fort) is an old seaport with narrow streets shaded by huge live oaks and lined with 18th-century homes. The oldest house (at Port Republic and New streets) was built in 1717. This was the second area in North America to be discovered by the Spanish (1520), the site of the first fort on the continent (1525), and the first attempted settlement (1562). Several forts have been excavated, dating from 1566 and 1577.

Beaufort has been used as a setting for several films, including *The Big Chill.* Scenes from the Paramount blockbuster *Forrest Gump,* starring Tom Hanks, and *The Prince of Tides* were also shot here.

GETTING THERE   If you're traveling from the north, take I-95 to Exit 33; then follow the signs to the center of Beaufort. From the south, take I-95 to Exit 8 and follow the signs. From Hilton Head, go on U.S. 278 west, and after N.C. 170 North joins U.S. 278, follow N.C. 170 into Beaufort.

VISITOR INFORMATION The **Beaufort Chamber of Commerce,** 1006 Bay St. (P.O. Box 910), Beaufort, SC 29901 (© **843/524-3163**), has information and self-guided tours of this historic town. It's open daily 9:30am to 5:30pm. If your plans are for early to mid-October, write the **Historic Beaufort Foundation,** P.O. Box 11, Beaufort, SC 29901 (© **843/524-6334**), for specific dates and detailed information about its 3 days of antebellum house and garden tours.

EXPLORING THE TOWN   A tour called **The Spirit of Old Beaufort,** 210 Scott's St. (© **843/525-0459**), takes you on a journey through the old town, exploring local history, architecture, horticulture, and Low Country life. You'll see houses that are not accessible on other tours. Your host, clad in period costume, will guide you for 2 hours from Tuesday to Saturday at 10am, 11:30am, 1:15pm, and 3:30pm. The cost is $15 for adults, $7 for children 12 and under. Tours depart from just behind the John Market Verdier House Museum (see below).

John Market Verdier House Museum, 801 Bay St. (© **843/524-6334**), is a restored 1802 house partially furnished to depict the life of a merchant planter during the period from 1800 to 1825. It's one of the best examples of the Federal period and was once known as the Lafayette Building, because the Marquis de Lafayette is said to have spoken here in 1825. It's open Monday to Saturday from 11am to 4pm, charging $4 for adults and $2 for children.

St. Helen's Episcopal Church, 501 Church St. (℅ **843/ 522-1722**), traces its origin back to 1712. Visitors, admitted free Monday to Saturday from 10am to 4pm, can see its classic interior and visit the graveyard, where tombstones served as operating tables during the Civil War.

Beaufort is also the home of the famous **U.S. Marine Corps Recruit Depot.** The visitor center (go to Building 283) is open daily from 10am to 4:30pm. You can take a driving tour or a bus tour (free) around the grounds, where you'll see an Iwo Jima monument; a monument to the Spanish settlement of Santa Elena (1521); and a memorial to Jean Ribaut, the Huguenot who founded Beaufort in 1562.

WHERE TO STAY

Beaufort Inn 🌟🌟   This is the most appealing hotel in Beaufort and the place where whatever movie star happens to be shooting a film in town is likely to stay. The woodwork and moldings inside are among the finest in Beaufort, and the circular, four-story staircase has been the subject of numerous photographs and architectural awards. The bedrooms, each decorated in brightly colored individual style, are conversation pieces. A wine bar, grill room, and rose garden are more recent additions.

809 Port Republic St., Beaufort, SC 29902. ℅ **843/521-9000.** Fax 843/521-9500. www.beaufortinn.com. E-mail: bftinn@hargray.com. 12 units. $125–$350 double. Rates include full gourmet breakfast. AE, DISC, MC, V. *In room:* A/C, TV, minibar.

Cuthbert House Inn 🌟🌟   One of the grand old B&Bs of South Carolina, this showcase Southern home was built in 1790 in classic style. The inn was remodeled shortly after the Civil War to take on a more Victorian aura, but its present owner, Sharon Groves, has worked to modernize it without sacrificing its grace or antiquity. Graffiti carved by Union soldiers can still be seen on the fireplace mantel in the Eastlake room. Bedrooms are elegantly furnished in Southern plantation style, and some have four-poster beds. The inn is filled with large parlors and sitting rooms, and has the spacious hallways and 12-foot ceilings that are characteristic of Greek Revival homes. Modern amenities and conveniences such as private baths have been tastefully tucked in. Some bathrooms have the old cast-iron soaking tubs. At breakfast in the conservatory, you can order such delights as Georgia ice cream (cheese grits) and freshly made breads.

1203 Bay St., Beaufort, SC 29901. ℅ **800/327-9275** or 843/521-1315. Fax 843/ 521-1314. www.cuthberthouseinn.com. E-mail: cuthbert@hargray.com. 6 units.

Mar–Nov $145–$225 double; Dec–Feb $125–$225 double, suites $195–$205 year-round. Rates include full breakfast and afternoon tea or refreshments. AE, DISC, MC, V. *In room:* A/C, TV, minibar.

The Rhett House Inn ★★★ This inn is certainly very popular, at least with Hollywood film crews. Because it was a site for *Forrest Gump, The Prince of Tides,* and *The Big Chill,* chances are that you've seen it before. It's a Mobil and AAA four-star inn in a restored 1820 Greek Revival plantation-type home. Rooms are furnished with English and American antiques, and ornamented with Oriental rugs; eight contain whirlpools. The veranda makes an ideal place to sit and view the gardens. The inn is open year-round. Children under 5 are not accepted.

1009 Craven St., Beaufort, SC 29902. (℃ **843/524-9030.** Fax 843/524-1310. www.rhetthouseinn.com. E-mail: rhetthse@hargray.com. 17 units. $150–$300 double. Rates include continental breakfast, afternoon tea, and evening hors d'oeuvres. AE, MC, V. Free parking. *In room:* A/C, TV.

Sea Island Inn This is a basic two-story motel with very reasonable rates for what you get. Few of the rooms have sea views; most overlook a small swimming pool, separated from the rest of the motel in a brick-sided courtyard. Although the rooms are nothing special, they're comfortable and clean.

1015 Bay St., Beaufort, SC 29902. (℃ **800/528-1234** or 843/522-2090. Fax 843/521-4858. www.bestwestern.com. 43 units. $89–$105 double. Rates include continental breakfast. AE, DC, DISC, MC, V. *In room:* A/C, TV.

Two Suns Inn When this place was built in 1917, it was one of the grandest homes in its prosperous neighborhood, offering views of the coastal road and the tidal flatlands beyond. Every imaginable modern (at the time) convenience was added, including a baseboard vacuum-cleaning system, an electric call box, and steam heat. Later, when it became housing for unmarried teachers in the public schools, the place ran down. But in 1990, a retired music teacher and band leader, Ron Kay, and his wife, Carroll, saw the inn—"an accident stop along the way to North Carolina," they say—bought it, and transformed it into a cozy B&B. Part of the inn's appeal stems from its lack of pretension, as a glance at the homey bedrooms and uncomplicated furnishings will show you.

1705 Bay St., Beaufort, SC 29902. (℃ **800/534-4244** or 843/522-1122. Fax 843/522-1122. www.twosunsinn.com. E-mail: twosuns@islc.net. 6 units. $133–$159 double. Rates include full breakfast and afternoon tea. AE, DC MC, V. *In room:* TV.

WHERE TO DINE

Beaufort Inn Restaurant ⚜ INTERNATIONAL   Stylish and urbane, and awash with colonial lowland references, this is the local choice for celebratory or business dinners, amid candlelit surrounds. Meat courses include chicken piccata with artichokes and sun-dried tomatoes, and an excellent grilled filet mignon with herbal Gorgonzola butter and shiitake mushrooms; vegetarian main courses include roasted-pepper-and-eggplant torte. On the menu is a variation on a dish whose invention has been claimed by a string of other restaurants in the South Carolina Low Country: crispy whole flounder with strawberry-watermelon chutney.

In the Beaufort Inn, 809 Port Republic St. ℭ **843/521-9000.** Reservations recommended. Main courses $21–$27.50. AE, MC, V. Mon–Sat 6–10pm, Sun 11am–2pm.

Emily's INTERNATIONAL   This is our favorite restaurant in Beaufort, a spot whose ambience and attitude put us in mind of Scandinavia. That's hardly surprising, because the bearded owner is an emigré from Sweden who feels comfortable in the South Carolina lowlands after years of life at sea. Some folks just go to the bar to sample tapas: miniature portions of tempura shrimp, fried scallops, stuffed peppers, and at least 50 others. Menu items might include cream of mussel and shrimp soup, rich enough for a main course; fillet "black and white" (fillets of beef and pork served with béarnaise sauce); duck with orange sauce; a meltingly tender Wiener schnitzel; and the catch of the day. Everything is served in stomach-stretching portions.

906 Port Republic St. ℭ **843/522-1866.** Reservations recommended. Tapas $7; main courses $20–$23. AE, DISC, MC, V. Drinks and tapas Mon–Sat 4–10pm; main courses Mon–Sat 6–10pm.

Olly's By the Bay SEAFOOD/STEAKHOUSE   This dead-center restaurant seems to change its stripes every other year or so. Today it's an informal haven, both a bar and restaurant. As management admits, we have "cooks only—no chefs," so you know what to expect. Nonetheless, you get some of the best steaks in the area, cooked to your specifications on the grill. A "shrimp burger" is the house specialty. The catch of the day can be broiled, blackened, or sautéed. Try the oyster sandwich or the golden scallops. To keep the menu a little diverse, a few pasta dishes are also offered.

822 Bay St. ℭ **843/524-2500.** Reservations recommended but not necessary. Main courses $12.95–$19.75; lunch $5.95–$14.95. AE, DC, DISC, MC, V. Mon–Sat 11am–3pm, 6–9pm.

4

Hilton Head: A Premier Southeast Resort

The largest sea island between New Jersey and Florida and one of America's great resort meccas, Hilton Head is surrounded by the Low Country, where much of the romance, beauty, and graciousness of the Old South survives. Broad white-sand beaches are warmed by the Gulf Stream and fringed with palm trees and rolling dunes. Palms mingle with live oaks, dogwood, and pines, and everything is draped in Spanish moss. Graceful sea oats, anchoring the beaches, wave in the wind. The subtropical climate makes all this beauty the ideal setting for golf and for some of the Southeast's finest saltwater fishing. Far more sophisticated and upscale than Myrtle Beach and the Grand Strand, Hilton Head's "plantations" (as most resort areas here call themselves) offer visitors something of the traditional leisurely lifestyle that's always held sway here.

Although it covers only 42 square miles (it's 12 miles long and 5 miles wide at its widest point), Hilton Head feels spacious, thanks to judicious planning from the beginning of its development in 1952. And that's a blessing, because about half a million resort guests visit annually (the permanent population is about 25,000). The broad beaches on its ocean side, sea marshes on the sound, and natural wooded areas of live and water oak, pine, bay, and palmetto trees in between have all been carefully preserved amid commercial explosion. This lovely setting attracts artists, writers, musicians, theater groups, and craftspeople. The only city (of sorts) is Harbour Town, at Sea Pines Plantation, a Mediterranean-style cluster of shops and restaurants.

1 Essentials

GETTING THERE It's easy to fly into Charleston, rent a car, and drive to Hilton Head (about 65 miles south of Charleston). See chapter 1 for complete details on all the airlines flying into Charleston. If you're driving from other points south or north, just exit off I-95 to reach the island (Exit 28 off I-95 south, Exit 5 off I-95 north). U.S. 278 leads over the bridge to the island. It's 52 miles northeast of Savannah and located directly on the Intracoastal Waterway.

VISITOR INFORMATION   The **Island Visitors Information Center** is on U.S. 278 at S.C. 46 (© **888/741-7666** or 843/785-4472; www.islandvisitorcenter.com), just before you cross over from the mainland. It offers a free *Where to Go* booklet, including a visitor map and guide. It's open daily from 9am to 6pm.

The **Hilton Head Visitors and Convention Bureau** (Chamber of Commerce), 1 Chamber Dr. (© **843/785-3673;** www.hilton headisland.org), offers free maps of the area and will assist you in finding places of interest and outdoor activities. It will not, however, make hotel reservations. It's open Monday to Friday from 8:30am to 5:30pm.

GETTING AROUND   U.S. 278 is the divided highway that runs the length of the island.

Yellow Cab (© **843/686-6666**) has flat two-passenger rates determined by zone, with an extra $2 charge for each additional person.

SPECIAL EVENTS   The earliest annual event is **Springfest,** a March festival featuring seafood, live music, stage shows, and tennis and golf tournaments. In early or mid-April, top tennis players congregate for the **Family Circle Magazine Cup Tennis Tournament,** held at the Sea Pines Racquet Club. Outstanding PGA golfers also descend on the island in mid-April for the **MCI Heritage Classic** at the Harbour Town Golf Links. To herald fall, the **Hilton Head Celebrity Golf Tournament** is held on Labor Day weekend at Palmetto Dunes and Sea Pines Plantation.

2 Where to Stay

Hilton Head has some of the finest hotel properties in the Deep South, and prices are high—unless you book into one of the motels run by national chains. Most facilities offer discount rates from November to March, and golf and tennis packages are available.

The most comprehensive central reservations service on the island, **The Vacation Company,** P.O. Box 5312, Hilton Head Island, SC 29938 (© **800/845-7018** in the United States and Canada; www.hiltonheadcentral.com), can book you into any hotel

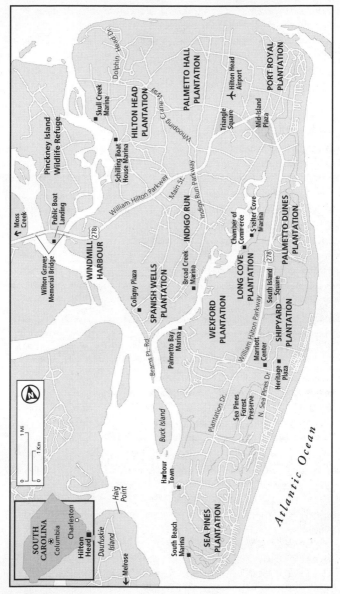

Port Royal Plantation
Palmetto Hall Plantation
Hilton Head Airport
Dolphin Head Dr.
Skull Creek Marina
Hilton Head Plantation
Whooping Crane Wy.
Mid-Island Plaza
Triangle Square
Pinckney Island Wildlife Refuge
Schilling Boat House Marina
Main St.
Chamber of Commerce
Shelter Cove Marina
Palmetto Dunes Plantation
Moss Creek
Public Boat Landing
William Hilton Parkway
Indigo Run Parkway
Indigo Run
Wilton Graves Memorial Bridge
Windmill Harbour
278
Spanish Wells Plantation
Coligny Plaza
Broad Creek Marina
Long Cove Plantation
South Island Square
278
Shipyard Plantation
Brams Pt. Rd.
Wexford Plantation
Palmetto Bay Marina
William Hilton Parkway
Marriott Center
Heritage Plaza
Plantation Dr.
Buck Island
Sea Pines Forest Preserve
N. Sea Pines Dr.
Harbour Town
Haig Point
South Carolina
Columbia
Charleston
Hilton Head
Daufuskie Island
Melrose
South Beach Marina
Sea Pines Plantation
Atlantic Ocean

1 Mi
1 Km

room or villa on the island at no charge. It's open Monday to Saturday from 9am to 5pm.

Another option is renting a private home, villa, or condo. Families might consider a villa rental if it fits into their budget. For up-to-date availability, rates, and bookings, contact **Island Rentals and Real Estate,** P.O. Box 5915, Hilton Head Island, SC 29938 (© **800/845-6134** or 843/785-3813). The toll-free number is in operation 24 hours, but office hours are Monday to Friday from 8:30am to 6pm, Saturday 8:30 to 11:30am and 2 to 5pm.

VERY EXPENSIVE

Hyatt Regency Hilton Head ⟨⟨ Lacking the pizzazz of the Westin (recommended below), this is the largest hotel on the island, set on two landscaped acres surrounded by the much-more massive acreage of Palmetto Dunes Plantation. The 10-story tower virtually dominates everything around it. Bedrooms are smaller and less opulent than you might expect of such a well-rated hotel, but their unremarkable decor is offset by balconies looking out over the gardens or the water.

In Palmetto Dunes Plantation (P.O. Box 6167), Hilton Head Island, SC 29938. © **800/55-HYATT** or 843/785-1234. Fax 843/842-4695. www.hyatthiltonhead. com. E-mail: Hyattresort@hargray.com. 505 units. $195–$275 double; $400–$850 suite. Parking $8. AE, DC, DISC, MC, V. **Amenities:** Hemingway's restaurant (see "Where to Dine," later in this chapter); a cabaret-style dining and drinking club; room service; babysitting; laundry; Camp Hyatt for children; outdoor pool and whirlpool; three 18-hole golf courses; 25 tennis courts, sailboats, and health club (with saunas, whirlpool, indoor pool, and exercise room). In room: A/C, TV.

Main Street Inn ⟨⟨ Don't expect cozy Americana from this small, luxurious inn, as it's grander and more European in its motifs than its name would imply. Designed like a small-scale villa that you might expect to see in the south of France, it was built in 1996 in a format that combines design elements from both New Orleans and Charleston, including cast-iron balustrades and a formal semi-tropical garden where guests are encouraged to indulge in afternoon tea. Inside, you'll find artfully clipped topiary, French provincial furnishings, and accommodations that are more luxurious, and more richly appointed, than any other hotel in Hilton Head. Color schemes throughout make ample use of golds, mauves, and taupes; floors are crafted from slabs of either stone or heart pine; fabrics are richly textured; and plumbing and bathroom fixtures are aggressively upscale. Overall, despite a location that requires a drive to the nearest beach, the hotel provides a luxe alternative to the less personalized megahotels that lie nearby. No children under 12 are admitted into this very adult property. AAA, incidentally, awarded it a much-coveted four-star rating. A garden overlooks one of the putting greens of the Bear Creek golf course.

2200 Main St., Hilton Head Island, SC 29926. ✆ **800/471-3001** or 843/681-3001. Fax 843/681-5541. www.mainstreetinn.com. 33 units. $185–275 double. $35 surcharge for third occupant of double room. Rates include breakfast and afternoon tea. Free parking. AE, DC, MC, V. **Amenities:** Breakfast; afternoon tea; 4-foot-deep lap pool in the garden; a whirlpool; small-scale spa, offering a limited array of massage, health, and beauty treatments. *In room:* A/C, TV.

Westin Resort 👧👧   Set near the isolated northern end of Hilton Head Island on 24 landscaped acres, this is the most opulent European-style hotel in town. Its Disneyesque design, including cupolas and postmodern ornamentation that looks vaguely Moorish, evokes fanciful Palm Beach hotels. If there's a drawback, it's the stiff formality. Adults accompanied by a gaggle of children and bathers in swimsuits will not necessarily feel comfortable in the reverently hushed corridors. The bedrooms, most of which have ocean views, are outfitted in Low Country plantation style, with touches of Asian art thrown in for additional glamour.

2 Grasslawn Ave., Hilton Head Island, SC 29928. ✆ **800/WWESTIN-1** or 843/681-4000. Fax 843/681-1087. www.westin.com. E-mail: tood.aaronson@ westin.com. 412 units. $195–$395 double; $500–$8600 suite. Children 17 and under stay free in parents' room; children 4 and under eat free. Special promotions offered. AE, DC, DISC, MC, V. **Amenities:** The Barony restaurant (see "Where to Dine," later in this chapter); poolside dining; seafood buffet restaurant; lounge; room service; babysitting; laundry; health club; three top-notch golf courses; Palm Beach–style racquet club with 16 tennis courts; palm-flanked swimming pool (with immediate access to a white-sand beach). *In room:* A/C, TV, minibar.

EXPENSIVE

Disney Hilton Head Island Resort 👧👧   This family-conscious resort is on a 15-acre island that rises above Hilton Head's widest estuary, Broad Creek. When it opened in 1996, it was the only U.S.–based Disney resort outside Florida and California. About 20 woodsy-looking buildings are arranged into a compound. Expect lots of pine trees and fallen pine needles, garlands of Spanish moss, plenty of families with children, and an ambience that's several notches less intense than that of hotels in Disney theme parks. Part of the fun, if you like this sort of thing in concentrated doses, are the many summer-camp-style activities. Public areas have outdoorsy colors (forest green and cranberry), stuffed game fish, and varnished pine. References are made to Shadow the Dog (a fictitious golden retriever that is the resort's mascot) and Mathilda (a maternal figure who conducts cooking lessons for children as part of the resort's planned activities). All accommodations contain mini-kitchens, suitable for feeding sandwiches and macaroni to the kids but hardly the kind of thing that a gourmet chef would enjoy, and wooden furniture that's consistent with the resort's vacation-home-in-the-forest theme. Children's activities usually last 90 to 120 minutes, giving parents a chance to be alone for a while. Programs include eco-tours with Disneyesque themes, arts and crafts, boat trips to look for dolphins, canoeing lessons, weenie roasts, marshmallow roasts with campfire song, and "unbirthday" celebrations for any adult or child who doesn't happen to be celebrating a birthday that day. Babysitting can be arranged for an extra fee. One of Hilton Head's most beautiful fishing piers allows easy access to whatever bites underwater.

22 Harbourside Lane, Hilton Head Island, SC 29928. ℂ **800/453-4911** or 843/341-4100. Fax 843/341-4130. www.dvcresorts.com. 31 studios, 88 villas. $105–$255 studio; $140–$330 1-bedroom villa, $160–$395 2-bedroom villa, $305–$675 3-bedroom villa. AE, MC, V. **Amenities:** Tide Me Over restaurant (lunch and breakfast); swimming pool with giant water slide; beach club (about a mile distant) includes direct access to the sands of Palmetto Cove, a second swimming pool, watersports, and a lunch-only snack bar (a shuttle bus makes frequent connections between the beach club and hotel daily between 8:30am and 5pm); deli and general store. *In room:* A/C, TV.

Hilton Head Crowne Plaza Resort 🏖

Tucked away within the Shipyard Plantation, and designed as the centerpiece of that plantation's 800 acres, this five-story inn gives its major competitor, Westin Resort, stiff competition. It underwent a $10 million renovation in 1993 and today has the island's most dignified lobby: a mahogany-sheathed postmodern interpretation of Chippendale decor. The golf course associated with the place has been praised by the National Audubon Society for its respect for local wildlife. Bedrooms are nothing out of the ordinary, yet the sheer beauty of the landscaping, the attentive service, the omnipresent nautical theme, and the well-trained staff (dressed in nautically inspired uniforms) can go a long way toward making your stay memorable.

130 Shipyard Dr., Shipyard Plantation, Hilton Head Island, SC 29928. ℂ **800/465-4329** or 843/842-2400. Fax 843/785-8463. www.crowneplaza.com. 340 units. $179–$207 double; $320–$520 suite. AE, DC, DISC, MC, V. **Amenities:** Three restaurants; Signals Lounge; room service; valet laundry and dry-cleaning service; meeting and conference rooms; concierge; car rental; leisure-activities desk; health club with sauna and whirlpool; outdoor covered pavilion; and indoor, outdoor, and children's pools; golf and tennis can be arranged. *In room:* A/C, TV, minibar.

Hilton Oceanfront Resort 🏵 This award-winning property isn't the most imposing on the island. Many visitors, however, prefer the Hilton because of its hideaway position: tucked in at the end of the main road through Palmetto Dunes. The low-rise design features hallways that open to sea breezes at either end. The bedrooms are some of the largest on the island, and balconies angling out toward the beach allow sea views from every accommodation.

23 Ocean Lane (P.O. Box 6165), Hilton Head Island, SC 29938. ℂ **800/345-8001** or 843/842-8000. Fax 843/341-8037. www.hilton.com. E-mail: hiltonhh@hargray. com. 324 units (with kitchenette). $190–$259 double; $350–$450 suite. AE, DC, DISC, MC, V. **Amenities:** Mostly Seafood is the resort's premier restaurant, although cafes and bars—and even a Pizza Hut on the grounds—serve less-expensive fare; room service; babysitting; laundry; children's vacation program (like a summer camp and the best on the island); modest health club; whirlpool; sauna; two outdoor pools; expansive sandy beach. *In room:* A/C, TV.

MODERATE

Holiday Inn Oceanfront 🏵 The island's leading motor hotel, across from Coligny Plaza, this five-story high-rise opens onto a quiet stretch of beach on the southern side of the island, near Shipyard Plantation. It's better than ever after a 1995 renovation. The rooms are spacious and well furnished, decorated in tropical pastels, but the balconies are generally too small for use. The upper floors have the views, so you should try for accommodations there. In summer, planned children's activities are offered. No-smoking and handicapped-accessible rooms are available.

(P.O. Box 5728), 1 S. Forest Beach Dr., Hilton Head Island, SC 29938. ℂ **800/ HOLIDAY** or 843/785-5126. Fax 843/785-6678. www.holiday-inn.com. 202 units. $79–$209 double; $250 suite. Parking $2. AE, DC, DISC, MC, V. *In room:* A/C, TV.

Radisson Suite Resort Set on the eastern edge of Hilton Head's main traffic artery, midway between the Palmetto Dunes and Shipyard plantations, this is a three-story complex of functionally furnished but comfortable one-bedroom suites. The setting is wooded and parklike, and both cost-conscious families and business travelers on extended stays appreciate the simple cooking facilities in each accommodation. Each unit has an icemaker, microwave, and coffeemaker. Limited resort facilities are on-site, including a swimming pool, a hot tub, and a cluster of lighted tennis courts.

12 Park Lane (in Central Park), Hilton Head Island, SC 29938. ℂ **800/333-3333** or 843/686-5700. Fax 843/686-3952. www.radisson.com. 156 units. Apr–Sept, $139–$149 suite. Oct–Mar, $89–$99 suite. Rates include continental breakfast. AE, DC, DISC, MC, V. *In room:* A/C, TV.

South Beach Marina Inn   Of the dozens of available accommodations in Sea Pines Plantation, this 1986 clapboard-sided complex
of marina-front buildings is the only place offering traditional hotel-
style rooms by the night. With lots of charm, despite its aggressive
theme, the inn meanders over a labyrinth of catwalks and stairways
above a complex of shops, souvenir kiosks, and restaurants. Each
unit is cozily outfitted with country-style braided rugs, pinewood
floors, and homespun-charm decor celebrating rural 19th-century
America. All units include a kitchenette.

In the Sea Pines Plantation, 232 S. Sea Pines Dr., Hilton Head Island, SC 29938.
𝒞 843/671-6498. www.southbeachvillage.com. 17 units. $109–$159 1-bedroom
apt; $169–$210 2-bedroom apt. AE, DISC, MC, V. *In room:* A/C, TV.

INEXPENSIVE

Fairfield Inn and Suites by Marriott   This three-story motel in
Shelter Cove has all the features of Marriott's budget chain, including complimentary coffee in the lobby, no-smoking rooms, and
same-day dry cleaning. The inn provides easy access to the beach,
golf, tennis, marinas, and shopping. The rooms are wheelchair-
accessible and, although they're unremarkable, they are a good value
for expensive Hilton Head. Families save extra money by using one
of the grills outside for a home-style barbecue, to be enjoyed at one
of the picnic tables. In addition, a heated pool is provided.

9 Marina Side Dr., Hilton Head Island, SC 29938. 𝒞 800/228-2800 or 843/
842-4800. Fax 843/842-4800. www.marriott.com. 119 units. $69–$79 double; $105
suite. Rates include continental breakfast. Children 17 and under stay free in parents' room. Senior discounts available. AE, DC, DISC, MC, V. *In room:* A/C, TV.

Hampton Inn   Although slightly edged out by its major competitor, the Fairfield Inn by Marriott, this is the second-most-sought-
after motel on Hilton Head, especially by families and business
travelers. It's 5 miles from the bridge and the closest motel to the
airport. Rooms in pastel pinks and greens are quite comfortable and
well maintained. Some units have refrigerators. Local calls are free,
and no-smoking rooms are available. A health spa features an
outdoor pool, whirlpool, and exercise equipment. A coin laundry is
on-site, and tennis and golf can be arranged. Bicycles can also be
rented.

1 Airport Rd., Hilton Head Island, SC 29926. 𝒞 800/HAMPTON or 843/681-7900.
Fax 843/681-4330. www.hampton-inn.com. 124 units (12 with kitchen units).
$69–$79 double. Children under 18 stay free in parents' room. Rates include continental breakfast. AE, DC, DISC, MC, V. *In room:* A/C, TV.

Quality Inn & Suites   Neck and neck with the Red Roof Inn, this motel attracts families watching their budgets. It's acceptable and clean in every way. Part of the Shoney empire, it offers basic bedrooms with streamlined modern furnishings. Some accommodations are reserved for nonsmokers and people with disabilities. Rooms have king-size or double beds and cable TVs. A large outdoor pool is on-site, and a Chinese restaurant is right next door. The restaurant serves breakfast, lunch, and dinner, and meals can be charged to your room. Golf and tennis can be arranged nearby.

Highway 278, 200 Museum St., Hilton Head Island, SC 29926. ℂ 843/342-7253. Fax 843/681-3655. www.qualityinnandsuites.com. 138 units. $68–$78 double. AE, DC, DISC, MC, V. *In room:* A/C, TV.

Red Roof Inn   Popular with families, this chain hotel is the island's budget special. Its rooms are basic motel-style, with king-size or double beds, but they're well maintained. Local calls are free, and Showtime is on the cable TVs. There's an outdoor pool, and public beaches and sports facilities are close at hand. The hotel is wheelchair-accessible.

5 Regency Pkwy. (off U.S. 278 between Palmetto Dunes and Shipyard Plantation), Hilton Head Island, SC 29938. ℂ 800/843-7663 or 843/686-6808. Fax 843/842-3352. www.redroof.com. 112 units. $59.99–$79.99 double; $129 suite. Rates include coffee and USA Today. AE, DC, DISC, MC, V. *In room:* A/C, TV.

VILLA RENTALS

Palmetto Dunes Resort ✿   This relaxed and informal enclave of privately owned villas is set within the sprawling 1,800-acre complex of Palmetto Dunes Plantation, 7 miles south of the bridge. Accommodations range all the way from rather standard hotel rooms, booked mostly by groups, to four-bedroom villas, each of the latter furnished in the owner's personal taste. This is the place for longer stays, ideal for families that want a home away from home when they're traveling. Villas are fully equipped and receive housekeeping service; they're located on the ocean, fairways, or lagoons. Each villa comes with a full kitchen, washer and dryer, living room and dining area, and balcony or patio.

Facilities include a tennis center with 25 courts, 5 golf courses, 3 miles of beach, 20 restaurants, a 10-mile lagoon ideal for canoeing, a playground, and a 200-slip marina.

(P.O. Box 5606) Palmetto Dunes, Hilton Head Island, SC 29938. ℂ 800/845-6130 or 843/785-1161. Fax 843/842-4482. www.palmettodunesresort.com. 500 units. $70–$155 double; $105–$225 villas and condos. Golf and honeymoon packages available. 2-night minimum stay. 50% deposit for reservations. AE, DC, DISC, MC, V. *In room:* A/C, TV.

Sea Pines Plantation   Since 1955, this has been one of the leading condo developments in America, sprawling across 5,500 acres at the southernmost tip of the island. Don't come to Sea Pines looking for a quick overnight accommodation. The entire place encourages stays of at least a week. Lodgings vary—everything from one- to four-bedroom villas to opulent private homes that are available when the owners are away. The clientele here includes hordes of golfers, because Sea Pines is the home of the MCI Classic, a major stop on the PGA tour. If you're not a Sea Pines guest, you can eat, shop, or enjoy some aspects of its nightlife, but there's a $5 entrance fee. For full details on this varied resort/residential complex, write for a free *Sea Pines Vacation* brochure.

Sea Pines (P.O. Box 7000), Hilton Head Island, SC 29938. ℂ 800/SEA-PINES or 843/785-3333. Fax 843/842-1475. www.seapines.com. 400 units (with kitchenette or kitchen). Year-round, $139–$235 1-bedroom villa; $157–$279 2-bedroom villa; $189–$319 3-bedroom villa. Rates are daily, based on 2-night stay. AE, DC, DISC, MC, V. *In room:* A/C, TV.

3 Where to Dine

VERY EXPENSIVE

The Barony ⓕ INTERNATIONAL   The Barony, quick to promote itself as the only AAA four-star restaurant on Hilton Head Island, didn't shy away from installing decor that's a hybrid between a stage set in Old Vienna and a brick-lined, two-fisted steakhouse. The lighting is suitably dim; the drinks are appropriately stiff; and as you dine in your plushly upholstered alcove, you can stare at what might be the largest wrought-iron chandelier in the state. The place caters to a resort-going crowd of casual diners. Everything is well prepared and in copious portions, although the chef doesn't experiment or stray far from a limited selection of tried-and-true steak-and-lobster fare. Your meal might include New York strip steak, tenderloin of pork with purée of mangos, lobster thermidor, or fresh Atlantic swordfish with pistachios.

In the Westin Resort, 2 Grass Lawn Ave. ℂ 843/681-4000. Reservations recommended. Main courses $25–$35. AE, DC, DISC, MC, V. Tues–Sat 5:30–10pm.

Hemingway's ⓕ SEAFOOD/INTERNATIONAL   This is the most upscale and charming hotel restaurant on the island. The dining experience here offers competent but unpretentious service and a nautical decor that includes a view of an exposed kitchen. The most worthwhile aspect of the menu is fresh fish cooked to perfection. Other choices include filet mignon, bullfighter-style paella, and very appealing charcoal-grilled poultry with lemon-thyme sauce. Your meal might be preceded by a frothy, rum-based tropical concoction flavored with coconut, banana, pineapple, and grenadine.

In the Hyatt Regency Hilton Head, Palmetto Dunes Resort. (C) **843/785-1234.** Reservations recommended. Main courses $22–$32. AE, DC, DISC, MC, V. Daily 5–11pm.

EXPENSIVE

Alexander's (R) INTERNATIONAL   One of the most visible independent restaurants (i.e., not associated with a hotel) on Hilton Head lies in a gray-stained, wood-sided building just inside the main entrance into Palmetto Dunes. You'll find a decor that includes Oriental carpets, big-windowed views over the salt marshes, wicker furniture, and an incongruous—some say startling—collection of vintage Harley Davidson motorcycles, none with more than 1,000 miles on them, dating from 1946, 1948, 1966, and 1993, respectively. Each is artfully displayed as a work of sculpture and as a catalyst to dialogues. Powerful flavors and a forthright approach to food are the rules of the kitchen. The chefs don't allow a lot of innovation on their menu—you've had all these dishes before—but fine ingredients are used, and each dish is prepared with discretion and restraint. Try the oysters Savannah or the bacon-wrapped shrimp and most definitely a bowl of Low Country seafood chowder. Guaranteed to set you salivating are the seafood pasta and the grilled Chilean sea bass in an herb vinaigrette. Steaks, duck, lamb, and pork—all in familiar versions—round out the menu.

76 Queen's Folly, Palmetto Dunes. (C) **843/785-4999.** Reservations recommended. Main courses $17.50–$24.95. AE, DC, MC, V. Daily 5–10pm.

Cattails INTERNATIONAL/MODERN AMERICAN   Locals come here for both the food and the international zest. With high ceilings and big windows, this is an airy setting, decorated with lace curtains and lots of hanging plants. Many of the dishes are inspired by Low Country traditions; others are more international or California in feeling and flair. Examples include roasted-eggplant, red-pepper, and mushroom focaccia; roasted-corn-and-crabmeat chowder; pan-seared flounder with South Carolina pecans and white-wine butter sauce; and tempting pastas, many of them made with seafood. The owners are Iranian-born Chef Mehdi Varedi and his American wife, Corinne, who directs a charming staff in the dining room. The restaurant's only drawback is its location: in a shopping center that's an inconvenient 17 miles north of the southern tip of the resort.

302 Moss Creek Village. © 843/837-7000. Reservations recommended. Main courses $15.50–$22.95. AE, DC, DISC, MC, V. Daily 6–10pm.

Charlie's L'Etoile Verte ✿✿ INTERNATIONAL Outfitted like a tongue-in-cheek version of a Parisian bistro, our favorite restaurant on Hilton Head Island was also a favorite with former President Clinton during one of his island conferences. The atmosphere is unpretentious but elegant, and it bursts with energy in an otherwise-sleepy shopping center. The service is attentive, polite, and infused with an appealingly hip mixture of old- and new-world courtesy. The kitchen has a narrow opening that allows guests to peep inside at the controlled hysteria. Begin with shrimp-stuffed ravioli, and move on to grilled tuna with a jalapeño beurre blanc (white butter) sauce, grilled quail with shiitake mushrooms and a Merlot sauce, or veal chops in peppercorn sauce. End this rare dining experience with biscotti or a "sailor's trifle." The wine list is impressive.

1000 Plantation Center. © 843/785-9277. Reservations required. Main courses $19–$28, lunch $9–$14. AE, DISC, MC, V. Tues–Sat 11:30am–2pm and 6–9pm.

MODERATE

Café Europa CONTINENTAL/SEAFOOD This fine European restaurant is at the base of the much-photographed Harbour Town Lighthouse, opening onto a panoramic view of Calibogue Sound and Daufuskie Island. In an informal, cheerful atmosphere, you can order fish that's poached, grilled, baked, or even fried. Baked Shrimp Daufuskie was inspired by local catches; it's stuffed with crab, green peppers, and onions. Grilled grouper is offered with a sauté of tomato, cucumber, dill, and white wine. Specialty dishes include a country-style chicken recipe from Charleston, with honey, fresh cream, and pecans. Tournedos au poivre is flambéed with brandy and simmered in a robust green-peppercorn sauce. The omelets, 14 in all, are perfectly prepared at breakfast (beginning at 10am) and are the island's finest. The bartender's Bloody Mary won an award as the island's best in a *Hilton Head News* contest.

Harbour Town, Sea Pines Plantation. © 843/671-3399. Reservations recommended for dinner. Main courses $17–$23, lunch $10–$12. AE, DC, MC, V. Daily 11am–2:30pm and 5:30–10pm.

Heritage Grill AMERICAN For years, this woodsy-looking refuge of golfers and their guests was open only to members of the nearby golf club. Several years ago, however, it opened to the public at large, a fact that's still not widely publicized in Hilton Head, and which sometimes seems to catch some local residents by surprise. Looking something like a postmodern version of a French château, this small-scale affair has views over the 9th hole and room for only about 50 diners at a time. Inside it's sporty-looking and relatively informal during the day, when most of the menu is devoted to thick-stuffed deli-style sandwiches and salads named in honor of golf stars who triumphed on the nearby golf course. Dinners are more formal and more elaborate, with good-tasting dishes such as local shrimp sautéed with ginger, Vidalia onions, and collard greens; roasted rack of American lamb with white beans, spinach, and rosemary; very fresh fish prepared any way you want; and an array of thick-cut slabs of meat that include beef, lamb, veal, and chicken.

In the Harbour Town Golf Links Clubhouse, Sea Pines. © 843/363-4080. Reservations recommended for dinner only. Lunch sandwiches and platters $7.95–$9.50; dinner main courses $18.50–$29.95. AE, DC, MC, V. Daily 11am–3pm; Wed–Sun 6–10pm.

Hudson's Seafood House on the Docks SEAFOOD Built as a seafood-processing factory in 1912, this restaurant still processes fish, clams, and oysters for local distribution, so you know that everything is fresh. If you're seated in the north dining room, you'll be eating in the original oyster factory. We strongly recommend the crab cakes, steamed shrimp, and the especially appealing blackened catch of the day. Local oysters (seasonal) are also a specialty, breaded and deep-fried. Before and after dinner, stroll on the docks past shrimp boats, and enjoy the view of the mainland and nearby Parris Island. Sunsets here are panoramic. Lunch is served in the Oyster Bar.

1 Hudson Rd. © 843/681-2772. Reservations not accepted. Main courses $14–$20, lunch $9–$13. AE, DC, MC, V. Daily 11am–2:30pm and 5–10pm. Go to Skull Creek just off Square Pope Rd. (signposted from U.S. 278).

Mostly Seafood SEAFOOD/AMERICAN The most elegant and innovative restaurant in the Hilton resort, it's noted for the way its chefs make imaginative dishes out of fresh seafood. Something about the decor—backlighting and glass-backed murals in designs of sea-green and blue—creates the illusion that you're floating in a boat. Menu items include fresh grouper, snapper, swordfish, flounder, salmon, trout, halibut, and pompano, prepared in any of seven ways. Dishes that consistently draw applause are corn-crusted filet of salmon with essence of hickory-smoked veal bacon and peach relish; and "fish in the bag," prepared with fresh grouper, scallops, and shrimp, laced with a dill-flavored cream sauce and baked in a brown paper bag.

In the Hilton Head Island Hilton Resort, in Palmetto Dunes Plantation. ⓒ **843/ 842-8000**. Reservations recommended. Main courses $14.95–$27. AE, DC, DISC, MC, V. Daily 5:30–10pm.

Neno's (Neno Il Toscano) ⭐ ITALIAN   One of the best restaurants on Hilton Head is incongruously tucked behind the big windows of what was originally conceived as a shop, inside a busy shopping mall, near a Wal-Mart store. Behind the white translucent curtains you'll find the airy, breezy kind of Italian restaurant you might have expected on southern Italy's Costa Smeralda. Amid mahogany and granite trim, and a mostly cream-colored decor, you can enjoy a rich inventory of summery dishes, with a menu that's enhanced by at least a dozen daily specials every day. Examples include thin-sliced veal served either with smoked prosciutto or with brandy, sausages, and mushrooms; charbroiled tuna on a bed of baked onions and herbs; and savory portobello mushrooms with goat cheese. Extensively promoted by the Food Network, this is the kind of place where well-heeled local residents come with friends and family to dine.

105 Festival Center, Rte. 278. ⓒ **843/342-2400**. Reservations recommended. Lunch main courses $8.95–$11.95; dinner main courses $13.95–$23.95. AE, MC, V. Mon–Fri 11:30am–2pm; Mon–Sat 6–10:30pm.

Santa Fe Café ⭐ MEXICAN   The best, most stylish Mexican restaurant on Hilton Head, it has rustic, Southwestern-inspired decor and cuisine that infuses traditional recipes with nouvelle flair. Menu items are often presented in colors as bright as the Painted Desert. Dishes might include tequila shrimp; herb-roasted chicken with jalapeño cornbread stuffing and mashed potatoes laced with red chiles; grilled tenderloin of pork with smoked habañero sauce and sweet-potato fries; and worthy burritos and chimichangas. The chiles rellenos are exceptional, stuffed with California goat cheese and sun-dried tomatoes. The quesadilla is one of the most beautifully presented dishes of any restaurant in town.

700 Plantation Center. ⓒ **843/785-3838**. Reservations recommended. Main courses $4.95–$7.95 at lunch, $14–$25 at dinner. AE, DISC, MC, V. Mon–Fri noon–2pm and daily 6–10pm.

INEXPENSIVE

The Crazy Crab North SEAFOOD   This is a branch of the chain that's most likely to be patronized by locals. In a modern, low-slung building near the bridge that connects the island with the South

Carolina mainland, it serves baked, broiled, or fried versions of stuffed flounder; seafood kebabs; oysters; the catch of the day; and any combination thereof. She-crab soup and New England–style clam chowder are prepared fresh daily; children's menus are available; and desserts are a high point for chocoholics.

U.S. 278 at Jarvis Creek. (C) **803/681-5021.** Reservations not accepted. Main courses $11.95–$22.95, lunch $6–$15. AE, DC, DISC, MC, V. Daily 11:30am–10pm.

Hofbrauhaus GERMAN   A sanitized German beer hall, this family favorite serves locals and visitors such national specialties as grilled bratwurst and smoked Westphalian ham, along with Wiener schnitzel and sauerbraten. One specialty that we like to order is roast duckling with spaetzle, red cabbage, and orange sauce. Note the stein and mug collection as you're deciding which of the large variety of German beers to order. A children's menu is available.

In the Pope Avenue Mall. (C) **843/785-3663.** Reservations recommended. Early-bird dinner (5–6:30pm only) $12.50; main courses $14–$21. AE, MC, V. Daily 5–10pm.

Taste of Thailand ⊛ THAI   Although this place is surpassed by its more glamorous neighbors, Charlie's and the Santa Fe Café, it does a bustling business with cost-conscious diners who appreciate the emphasis on exotic curries, lemongrass, and coconuts. Among scattered examples of Thai woodcarvings and handicrafts, you can enjoy a choice but limited menu offering beef, pork, chicken, shrimp, mussels, or tofu in a choice of different flavors. One of our favorites is chicken with stir-fried vegetables, Thai basil, and oyster sauce. The hottest dish is the green curry, but equally delectable is the curry with roasted peanuts and red chilies flavored with cumin seeds. Cold Thai spring rolls appear as an appetizer. A hot and sour soup is always on the menu, as is a spicy squid salad.

Plantation Center, 807 William Hilton Parkway. (C) **843/341-6500.** Reservations recommended. Lunch main courses $5–$8; dinner main courses $12–$17. AE, DC, MC, V. Tues–Fri 11:30am–2pm and 5–11pm.

4 Beaches, Golf, Tennis & Other Outdoor Pursuits

You can have an active vacation here any time of year; Hilton Head's subtropical climate ranges in temperature from the 50s in winter to the mid-80s in summer. And if you've had your fill of historic sights in Savannah or Charleston, don't worry—Hilton Head's attractions mainly consist of nature preserves, beaches, and other places to play.

The **Coastal Discovery Museum of Hilton Head,** 100 William Hilton Pkwy. ((C) **843/689-6767**), hosts 15 separate walks and guided tours. Tours go along island beaches and explore the salt marshes, stopping at Native American sites and the ruins of old forts or long-gone plantations. Most of the emphasis will be on the ecology of local plants and animals. There are no fees for this service; instead a donation of $2 is requested. Hours are Monday to Saturday 9am to 5pm, Sunday 10am to 3pm.

BEACHES   *Travel & Leisure* ranked Hilton Head's beaches as among the most beautiful in the world, and we concur. The sands are extremely firm, providing a sound surface for biking, hiking, jogging, and beach games. In summer, watch for the endangered loggerhead turtles that lumber ashore at night to bury their eggs.

All beaches on Hilton Head are public. Land bordering the beaches, however, is private property. Most beaches are safe, although there's sometimes an undertow at the northern end of the island. Lifeguards are posted only at major beaches, and concessions are available to rent beach chairs, umbrellas, and watersports equipment.

There are four public entrances to Hilton Head's beaches. The main parking and changing areas are on Folly Field Road, off U.S. 278 (the main highway), and at Coligny Circle, close to the Holiday Inn. Other entrances (signposted) from U.S. 278 lead to Singleton and Bradley beaches.

Most frequently used is **North and South Forest Beach,** adjacent to Coligny Circle (enter from Pope Avenue across from Lagoon Road). You'll have to use the parking lot opposite the Holiday Inn, paying a $4 daily fee until after 4pm. The adjacent Beach Park has toilets and a changing area, as well as showers, vending machines, and phones. It's a family favorite.

Of the beaches on the island's north, we prefer **Folly Field Beach.** Toilets, changing facilities, and parking are available.

GOLF   With 22 challenging golf courses on the island and an additional nine within a 30-minute drive, this is heaven for both professional and novice golfers. Some of golf's most celebrated architects—including George and Tom Fazio, Robert Trent Jones, Pete Dye, and Jack Nicklaus—have designed championship courses on the island. Wide, scenic fairways and rolling greens have earned Hilton Head the reputation of being the resort with the most courses on the "World's Best" list.

Many of Hilton Head's championship courses are open to the public, including the **George Fazio Course** at Palmetto Dunes

Resort (© **843/785-1130**), an 18-hole, 6,534-yard, par-70 course that *Golf Digest* ranked in the top 50 of its "75 Best American Resort Courses." The course has been cited for its combined length and keen accuracy. The cost is $90 for 18 holes, and hours are daily from 6:30am to 6:30pm.

Old South Golf Links, 50 Buckingham Plantation Dr., Bluffton (© **800/257-8997** or 843/785-5353), is an 18-hole, 6,772-yard, par-72 course, open daily from 7:30am to 7pm. It's recognized as one of the "Top 10 New Public Courses" by *Golf Digest*, which cites its panoramic views and setting ranging from an oak forest to tidal salt marshes. Greens fees range from $62 to $75. The course lies on Highway 278, 1 mile before the bridge leading to Hilton Head.

Hilton Head National, Highway 278 (© **843/842-5900**), is a Gary Player Signature Golf Course, including a full-service pro shop and a grill and driving range. It's an 18-hole, 6,779-yard, par-72 course with gorgeous scenery that evokes Scotland. Greens fees range from $50 to $64, and hours are daily 7:45am to 6:30pm. A regulation 9-hole course was added in 1999. Greens fees on this course are $34.

Island West Golf Club, Highway 278 (© **843/689-6660**), was nominated in 1992 by *Golf Digest* as the best new course of the year. With its backdrop of oaks, elevated tees, and rolling fairways, it's a challenging but playable 18-hole, 6,803-yard, par-72 course. Greens fees range from $40 to $56, and hours are from 7am to 6pm daily.

Robert Trent Jones Course at the Palmetto Dunes Resort (© **843/785-1138**) is an 18-hole, 6,710-yard, par-72 course with a winding lagoon system that comes into play on 11 holes. The greens fees are $90 to $130 for 18 holes, and hours are daily from 7am to 6pm.

TENNIS   *Tennis* magazine ranked Hilton Head among its "50 Greatest U.S. Tennis Resorts." No other domestic destination can boast such a concentration of tennis facilities: more than 300 courts that are ideal for beginners, intermediate, and advanced players. The island has 19 tennis clubs, 7 of which are open to the public. A wide variety of tennis clinics and daily lessons are available.

Sea Pines Racquet Club, Sea Pines Plantation (© **843/363-4495**), has been ranked by *Tennis* magazine as a top-50 resort and was selected by the *Robb Report* as the best tennis resort in the United States. The club has been the site of more nationally televised tennis events than any other location, and it's the home of

The Family Circle Magazine Cup Women's Tennis Championships. Two hours of tennis is complimentary for guests of the hotel; otherwise, there's a $20-per-hour charge. The club has 25 clay and 5 hard courts (hard courts are lighted for night play).

Port Royal Racquet Club, Port Royal Plantation (✆ **843/686-8803**), offers 10 clay and 4 hard courts, plus 2 natural-grass courts. Night games are possible on all courts. Charges range from $18 to $20 per hour, and reservations should be made a day in advance. Clinics are $18 per hour.

Hilton Head Island Beach and Tennis Resort, 40 Folly Field Rd. (✆ **843/842-4402**), features a dozen lighted hard courts, costing only $15 per hour.

Palmetto Dunes Tennis Center, Palmetto Dunes Resort (✆ **843/785-1152**), has 19 clay, 2 hard, and 4 artificial-grass courts (some lighted for night play). Hotel guests pay $20 per hour; otherwise, the charge is $25 per hour.

OTHER OUTDOOR PURSUITS

BIKING   Enjoy Hilton Head's 25 miles of bicycle paths, but stay off U.S. 278, the main artery, which has far too much traffic. Some beaches are firm enough to support wheels, and every year, cyclists seem to delight in dodging the waves or racing the fast-swimming dolphins in the nearby water.

Most hotels and resorts rent bikes to guests. If yours doesn't, try **Hilton Head Bicycle Company,** off Sea Pines Circle at 11B Archer Dr. (✆ **843/686-6888**). The cost is $12 per day, but only $18 for 3 days. Baskets, child carriers, locks, and headgear are supplied, and the inventory includes cruisers, BMXs, mountain bikes, and tandems. Hours are daily 9am to 5pm.

Another rental place is **South Beach Cycles,** South Beach Marina Village in Sea Pines (✆ **843/671-2453**), offering beach cruisers, tandems, child carriers, and bikes for kids. There's free delivery islandwide. Cost is $8 per half-day, $12 for a full day, or $19 for 3 days. Hours are 9am to 6pm daily.

HORSEBACK RIDING   Riding through beautiful maritime forests and nature preserves is reason enough to visit Hilton Head. We like **Lawton Fields Stables,** 190 Greenwood Dr., Sea Pines (✆ **843/671-2586**), offering rides for both adults and kids (kids ride ponies) through the Sea Pines Forest Preserve. The cost is $30 per person for a ride that lasts somewhat longer than an hour. Reservations are necessary.

JOGGING   Our favorite place for jogging is Harbour Town at Sea Pines. Go for a run through the town just as the sun is going down. Later, you can explore the marina and have a refreshing drink at one of the many outdoor cafes. In addition, the island offers lots of paved paths and trails that cut through scenic areas. Jogging along U.S. 278, the main artery, can be dangerous because of heavy traffic, however.

NATURE PRESERVES   The **Audubon-Newhall Preserve,** Palmetto Bay Road (© **843/689-2989**), is a 50-acre preserve on the south end of the island. Here, you can walk along marked trails to observe wildlife in its native habitat. Guided tours are available when plants are blooming. Except for public toilets, there are no amenities. The preserve is open from sunrise to sunset; admission is free.

The second-leading preserve is also on the south end of the island. **Sea Pines Forest Preserve,** Sea Pines Plantation (© **843/671-6486**), is a 605-acre public wilderness with marked walking trails. Nearly all the birds and animals known to live on Hilton Head can be seen here. (Yes, there are alligators, but there are also less fearsome creatures, such as egrets, herons, osprey, and white-tailed deer.) All trails lead to public picnic areas in the center of the forest. The preserve is open from sunrise to sunset year-round, except during the Heritage Golf Classic in early April. Maps and toilets are available.

WATERSPORTS

CRUISES & TOURS   To explore Hilton Head's waters, contact **Adventure Cruises, Inc.,** Shelter Cove Harbour, Suite G, Harbourside III (© **843/785-4558**). Outings include a nature cruise to Daufuskie Island (made famous by Pat Conroy's book *The Water Is Wide* and the film *Conrack*), with a guided safari on a jungle bus. The cost is adults $15 and children $7.50 round-trip. Departures are daily at 12:15pm, with a return to Hilton Head at 4:45pm.

Other popular cruises include a 1½-hour dolphin-watch cruise, which costs adults $16 and children $6. A 3-hour sunset dinner cruise aboard the vessel *Adventure* costs adults $34 and children $17, including an all-you-can-eat buffet.

FISHING   No license is needed for saltwater fishing, although freshwater licenses are required for the island's lakes and ponds. The season for fishing offshore is from April through October. Inland

⟲ Hilton Head's Wonderful Wildlife

Hilton Head has preserved more of its wildlife than almost any other resort destination on the East Coast.

Hilton Head Island's alligators are a prosperous lot, and in fact, the South Carolina Department of Wildlife and Marine Resources uses the island as a resource for repopulating state parks and preserves in which alligators' numbers have greatly diminished. The creatures represent no danger if you stay at a respectful distance. (Strange as it may seem, some unsuspecting tourists, thinking that the dead-still alligators are props left over from Disney, often approach the reptiles and hit them or kick at them—obviously, not a very good idea.)

Many of the large water birds that regularly grace the pages of nature magazines are natives of the island. The island's Audubon Society reports around 200 species of birds every year in its annual bird count, and more than 350 species have been sighted on the island during the past decade. The snowy egret, the large blue heron, and the osprey are among the most noticeable. Here, too, you may see the white ibis, with its strange beak that curves down, plus the smaller cattle egret, which first arrived on Hilton Head Island in 1954 from a South American habitat. They follow the island's cows, horses, and tractors to snatch grasshoppers and other insects.

A big part of the native story includes deer, bobcat, loggerhead turtles, otter, mink, and even a few wild boars. The bobcats are difficult to see, lurking in the deepest recesses of the forest preserves and in the undeveloped parts of the

fishing is good between September and December. Crabbing is also popular; crabs are easy to catch in low water from docks, boats, or right off a bank.

Off Hilton Head, you can go deep-sea fishing for amberjack, barracuda, shark, and king mackerel. Many rentals are available; we've recommended only those that have the best track records. Foremost is **A Fishin' Mission,** 145 Squire Pope Rd. (© **843/785-9177**), captained by Charles Getsinger aboard his 34-foot *Sportsfish*. Ice, bait, and tackle are included. Reservations are needed 1 to 2 days in island. The deer, however, are easier to encounter. One of the best places to watch these timid creatures is Sea Pines Plantation, on the southern end of the island. With foresight, the planners of this plantation set aside areas for deer habitat back in the 1950s, when the island master plan was conceived.

The loggerhead turtle, an endangered species, nests extensively along Hilton Head's 12 miles of wide, sandy beaches. Because the turtles choose the darkest hours of the night to crawl ashore and bury eggs in the soft sand, few visitors meet these 200-pound giants.

Ever-present is the bottlenosed dolphin, usually called a porpoise by those who are not familiar with the island's sea life. Hilton Head Plantation and Port Royal Plantation adjacent to Port Royal Sound are good places to meet up with the playful dolphins, as are Palmetto Dunes, Forest Beach, and all other oceanfront locations. In the summer, dolphins are inclined to feed on small fish and sea creatures very close to shore. Island beaches are popular with bikers, and this often offers a real point of interest for curious dolphins, who sometimes seem to swim along with the riders. Several excursion boats offer tours that provide an opportunity for fellowship with dolphins. Shrimp boats are a guaranteed point of congregation for the hungry guys.

The Sea Pines Forest Preserve, the Audubon-Newhall Preserve, and the Pinckney Island Wildlife Preserve, just off the island between the bridges, are of interest to nature lovers. The Museum of Hilton Head hosts several guided nature tours; call 𝒞 **843/689-6767**. Tours conducted Tuesday to Thursday, cost $10 for adults and $5 for children.

advance. The craft carries up to six people. The cost is $325 for a half-day, $475 for three-quarters of a day, $630 for a full day, or $250 for an evening trip (6-9pm).

Harbour Town Yacht Basin, Harbour Town Marina (𝒞 **843/ 671-2704**), has four boats of various sizes and prices. *The Manatee,* a 40-foot vessel, can carry a group of 8 to 15. The rates, set for 6 passengers, are $340 for 4 hours, $475 for 6 hours, and $680 for 8 hours. A charge of $15 per hour is added for each additional passenger.

The Hero and *The Echo* are 32-foot ships. Their rates for a group of 6 are $325 for 4 hours, $435 for 6 hours, and $550 for 8 hours. A smaller 3-passenger inshore boat is priced at $250 for 4 hours, $375 for 6 hours, and $500 for 8 hours.

A cheaper way to go deep-sea fishing—only $40 per person—is aboard *The Drifter* (© **843/671-3060**), a party boat that departs from the South Beach Marina Village. Ocean-bottom fishing is possible at an artificial reef 12 miles offshore.

KAYAK TOURS Eco-Kayak Tours, Palmetto Bay Marina (© **843/785-7131**), operates guided tours in Broad Creek. About four to five trips are offered each day; the cost is $30 to $50 per person, and anyone age 7 to 82 is welcome to participate. The Eco-Explorer outing begins at 8:30am; the excursion lasts 1½ hours and costs $20 for adults and $18 for children under 12. The tour explores the South Carolina Low Country environment, and you'll see local wildlife along the way.

Outside Hilton Head, the **Plaza at Shelter Cove** (© **843/686-6996**) and **South Beach Marina Village** (© **843/671-2643**) allow you to tour Low Country waterways by kayak. A 2-hour Dolphin Nature Tour costs $35 (half-price for children under 12). The tour takes you through the salt-marsh creeks of the Calibogue Sound or Pinckney Island Wildlife Refuge. The trip begins with brief instructions on how to control your boat. The Off-Island Day Excursion, at $60 per person, for 6 hours, or $48 for 4 hours, takes you along the Carolina barrier islands and the surrounding marsh-lands. These trips last 6 to 8 hours and include lunch.

PARASAILING Para-Sail Hilton Head, Harbour Town (© **843/671-4386**), takes you in a Sea Rocket powerboat for parasailing daily from 8am to 6:15pm. The cost is $45 per person for 400 feet of line or $55 for 700 feet of line, and reservations are necessary. Catamaran rides for up to six passengers are also featured, and sailing lessons are offered.

SAILING *Pauhana* and *Flying Circus,* Palmetto Bay Marina (© **843/686-2582**), are two charter sailboats on Hilton Head piloted by Capt. Jeanne Zailckas. You can pack a picnic lunch and bring your cooler aboard for a 2-hour trip—in the morning or afternoon, or at sunset. The cost is $20 for adults and $15 for children. Flying Circus offers private 2-hour trips for up to 6 people, costing $150.

Harbour Town Yacht Basin (© **843/363-2628**), offers both rentals and charters for sailing. Rental prices range from $175 to

$389 for 3 to 8 hours. Charters range from $110 to $135 for 2 hours. Dolphin, sunset, and evening cruises are available. Reservations are suggested.

WINDSURFING   Hilton Head is not recommended as a wind-surfing destination. Finding a place to windsurf is quite difficult, and one windsurfer warns that catching a tailwind at the public beaches at the airport and the Holiday Inn could land you at the bombing range on Parris Island, the Marine Corps' basic-training facility. Your resort may have equipment for rent, although what's usually available has been described as antiquated.

SHOPPING

Hilton Head is browsing heaven, with more than 30 shopping centers spread around the island. Chief shopping sites include **Pinelawn Mall** (Matthews Drive and U.S. 278), with more than 30 shops and half a dozen restaurants; and **Coligny Plaza** (Coligny Circle), with more than 60 shops, a movie theater, food stands, and several good restaurants. We've found some of the best bargains in the South at **Low Country Factory Outlet Village** (© 843/837-4339), on Highway 278 at the gateway to Hilton Head. The outlet has more than 45 factory stores, including Ralph Lauren, Brooks Brothers, and J. Crew. The hours of most shops are Monday to Saturday from 10am to 9pm and Sunday from 11am to 6pm.

5 Hilton Head After Dark

Hilton Head doesn't have Myrtle Beach's nightlife, but enough is here, centered mainly in hotels and resorts. Casual dress (but not swimming attire) is acceptable in most clubs.

Cultural interest focuses on the **Hilton Head Playhouse,** in the Self Family Arts Center, 14 Shelter Cove Lane (© 843/842-ARTS), which enjoys one of the best theatrical reputations in the Southeast. Hilton Head Playhouse Productions and other groups are sponsored at two venues. The Elizabeth Wallace Theater, a 350-seat, state-of-the-art theater, was added to the multiplex in 1996. The older Dunnagan's Alley Theater is located in a renovated warehouse. A range of musicals, contemporary comedies, and classic dramas is presented. Show times are 8pm Tuesday to Saturday, with a Sunday matinee at 2pm. Adult ticket prices range from $45 for a musical to $20 for a play. Children 16 and under are charged $8 to $15.

Quarterdeck   Our favorite waterfront lounge is the best place on the island to watch sunsets, but you can visit at any time during the afternoon and in the evening until 2am. Try to go early and grab one of the outdoor rocking chairs to prepare yourself for nature's light show. There's dancing every night to beach music and top-40 hits. Open daily 9am–10pm. Harbour Town, Sea Pines Plantation. ✆ 843/671-2222.

Remy's   Got the munchies? At Remy's, you can devour buckets of oysters or shrimp, served with the inevitable fries. The setting is rustic and raffish, and live music is provided. Open daily 11am to 4am. 28 Arrow Rd. ✆ 843/842-3800.

The Salty Dog Cafe   Locals used to keep this laid-back place near the beach to themselves, but now more and more visitors are showing up. Soft guitar music or Jimmy Buffett is often played. Dress is casual. Sit under one of the sycamores, enjoying your choice of food from an outdoor grill or buffet. Open daily till 2am. South Beach Marina. ✆ 843/671-2233.

Signals   In this upscale resort, you can enjoy live bands (often, 1940s golden oldies), along with R&B, blues, and jazz. The dance floor is generally crowded. Live bands perform Tuesday to Sunday from 9pm to 1am, and live jazz is presented on Monday from 6 to 9:30pm. A Sunday jazz brunch is held from 11am to 1:30pm. In the Crowne Plaza Resort, 130 Shipyard Dr. ✆ 843/842-2400.

5

Savannah: Mint Juleps & Magnolias

If you have time to visit only one city in the Southeast, make it Savannah. It's that special.

The movie *Forrest Gump* may have put the city squarely on the tourist map, but nothing changed the face of Savannah more than the 1994 publication of John Berendt's *Midnight in the Garden of Good and Evil*. The impact has been unprecedented, bringing in countless millions in revenue as thousands flock to see the sights from the mega-bestseller and the 1997 movie directed by Clint Eastwood. In fact, Savannah tourism has increased some 46% since publication of what's known locally as The Book. Many locals now earn their living off The Book's fallout, hawking postcards, walking tours, T-shirts, and in some cases their own careers, as in the case of the Lady Chablis, the black drag queen depicted in The Book who played herself in the Eastwood film (see below for the Lady's websites).

"What's special about Savannah?" we asked an old-timer. "Why, here we even have water fountains for dogs," he said.

The free spirit, the passion, and even the decadence of Savannah resembles that of Key West or New Orleans more than the Bible Belt down-home interior of Georgia. In that sense, it's as different from the rest of the state as New York City is from upstate New York.

Savannah—pronounce it with a drawl—conjures up all the clichéd images of the Deep South: live oaks dripping with Spanish moss, stately antebellum mansions, mint juleps sipped on the veranda, magnolia trees, peaceful marshes, horse-drawn carriages, ships sailing up the river (though no longer laden with cotton), and even General Sherman, no one's favorite military hero here.

Today, the economy and much of the city's day-to-day life still revolve around port activity. For the visitor, however, it's Old Savannah, a beautifully restored and maintained historic area, that's the big draw. For this we can thank seven Savannah ladies who, after watching mansion after mansion demolished in the name of progress, managed in 1954 to raise funds to buy the dilapidated Isaiah Davenport House—just hours before it was slated for demolition to make way for a parking lot. The women banded together as the Historic Savannah Foundation, then went to work buying up architecturally valuable buildings and reselling them to private owners who'd promise to restore them. As a result, more than 800 of Old Savannah's 1,100 historic buildings have been restored, using original paint colors—pinks and reds and blues and greens. This "living museum" is now the largest urban National Historic Landmark District in the country—some 2½ square miles, including 20 1-acre squares that still survive from Gen. James Oglethorpe's dream of a gracious city.

1 Essentials

ARRIVING

BY PLANE **Savannah International Airport** is about 8 miles west of downtown just off I-16. **American** (© **800/433-7300;** www.aa.com), **Delta** (© **800/221-1212;** www.delta.com), **United** (© **800/241/6522;** www.ual.com), and **US Airways** (© **800/ 428-4322;** www.usairways.com) have flights from Atlanta and Charlotte, with connections from other points.

 Limousine service to downtown locations (© **912/966-5364**) costs $16 one-way. The taxi fare is $20 for one person and $11 for each extra passenger.

BY CAR From north or south, I-95 passes 10 miles west of Savannah, with several exits to the city, and U.S. 17 runs through the city. From the west, I-16 ends in downtown Savannah and U.S. 80 also runs through the city from east to west. AAA services are available through the **AAA Auto Club South,** 712 Mall Blvd., Savannah, GA 31406 (© **912/352-8222;** www.aaa.com).

BY TRAIN The **train station** is at 2611 Seaboard Coastline Dr. (© **912/234-2611**), some 4 miles southwest of downtown; cab fare into the city is around $4. For **Amtrak** schedule and fare information, call © **800/USA-RAIL.**

VISITOR INFORMATION

The **Savannah Visitor Center,** 301 Martin Luther King Jr. Blvd., Savannah, GA 31401 (© **912/944-0455**), is open Monday to

Friday 8:30am to 5pm and Saturday and Sunday 9am to 5pm. The staff is friendly and efficient. Offered here are an audiovisual presentation costing $1.50 for adults and $1 for children, organized tours, and self-guided walking, driving, or bike tours with excellent maps, cassette tapes, and brochures.

Tourist information is also available from the **Savannah Area Convention & Visitors Bureau,** 101 East Bay St., Savannah, GA 31402 (*C* **800/444-2427** or 912/944-0456; www.savannah-visit. com). For information on current happenings, call *C* **912/ 233-ARTS.**

For everything you might want to know about The Book, check out the following Internet site: www.midnightinthegarden.com.

CITY LAYOUT

Every other street—north, south, west, and east—is punctuated by greenery. The grid of **21 scenic squares** was laid out in 1733 by Gen. James Oglethorpe, the founder of Georgia. The design—still in use—has been called "one of the world's most revered city plans." It's said that if Savannah didn't have its history and architecture, it would be worth a visit just to see the city layout.

Bull Street is the dividing line between east and west. On the south side are odd-numbered buildings, with even street numbers falling on the north side.

NEIGHBORHOODS IN BRIEF

Historic District   The Historic District—the real reason to visit Savannah—takes in both the riverfront and the City Market, described below. It's bordered by the Savannah River and Forsyth Park at Gaston Street and Montgomery and Price streets. Within its borders are more than 2,350 architecturally and historically significant buildings in a 2½-square-mile area. About 75% of these buildings have been restored.

Riverfront   In this most popular tourist district, River Street borders the Savannah River. Once lined with warehouses holding King Cotton, it has been the subject of massive urban renewal, turning this strip into a row of restaurants, art galleries, shops, and bars. The source of the area's growth was the river, which offered a prime shipping avenue for New World goods shipped to European ports. In 1818, about half of Savannah fell under quarantine during a yellow fever epidemic. River Street never fully recovered and fell into disrepair until its rediscovery in the mid-1970s. The urban-renewal project stabilized the downtown and revitalized the Historic District. Stroll the bluffs along the river on the old passageway of alleys, cobblestone walkways, and bridges known as **Factor's Walk.**

City Market   Two blocks from River Street and bordering the Savannah River, the City Market was the former social and business Mecca of Savannah. Since the late 18th century, it has known fires and various devastations, including the threat of demolition. But in a major move, the city of Savannah decided to save the district. Today, former decaying warehouses are filled with restaurants and shops offering everything from antiques to various collectibles, including many Savannah-made products. And everything from seafood and pizza to French and Italian cuisine is served here. Live music often fills the nighttime air. Some of the best jazz in the city is presented here in various clubs. The market lies at Jefferson and West Julian streets, bounded by Franklin Square on its western flank and Ellis Square on its eastern.

Victorian District   The Victorian District, south of the Historic District, holds some of the finest examples of post–Civil War architecture in the Deep South. The district is bounded by Martin Luther King Jr. Blvd. and East Broad, Gwinnett, and Anderson streets. Houses in the district are characterized by gingerbread trim, stained-glass windows, and imaginative architectural details. In all, the district encompasses an area of nearly 50 blocks, spread across some 165 acres. The entire district was listed on the National Register of Historic Places in 1974. Most of the two-story homes are wood frame and were constructed in the late 1800s on brick foundations. The district, overflowing from the historic inner core, became the first suburb of Savannah.

2 Getting Around

The grid-shaped Historic District is best seen on foot—the real point of your visit is to take leisurely strolls with frequent stops in the many squares.

BY CAR   Though you can reach many points of interest outside the Historic District by bus, your own wheels will be much more convenient, and they're absolutely essential for sightseeing outside the city proper.

All major car-rental firms have branches in Savannah and at the airport, including **Hertz** (© 800/654-3131, or 912/964-9595 at the airport); **Avis** (✆ 800/831-2847), with locations at 422 Airways Ave. (✆ 912/964-1781) and at 2215 Travis Field Rd. (✆ 912/964-0234); and **Budget** (✆ 800/527-0700), with offices at 7070 Abercorn St. (✆ 912/966-1771).

BY BUS   You'll need exact change for the 75¢ fare, plus 75¢ for a transfer. For route and schedule information, call **Chatham Area Transit (CAT)** at ✆ **912/233-5767.**

BY TAXI   The base rate for taxis is 60¢, with a $1.20 additional charge for each mile. For 24-hr. taxi service, call **Adam Cab Co.** at ✆ **912/927-7466.**

✆ *FAST FACTS:* Savannah

American Express   The American Express office has closed, but cardholders can obtain assistance by calling ✆ **800/221-7282.**

Dentists   Call Abercorn South Side Dental, 11139 Abercorn St., Suite 8 (✆ **912/925-9190**), for complete dental care and emergencies, Monday to Friday 8:30am to 3pm.

Drugstores   Drugstores are scattered throughout Savannah. One with longer hours is CVS, 11607 Abercorn St. (✆ **912/925-5568**), open Monday to Saturday 8am to midnight and Sunday 10am to 8pm.

Emergencies   Dial ✆ **911** for police, ambulance, or fire emergencies.

Hospitals   There are 24-hr. emergency-room services at Candler General Hospital, 5353 Reynolds St. (✆ **912/692-6637**), and the Memorial Medical Center, 4800 Waters Ave. (✆ **912/350-8390**).

Newspapers   The *Savannah Morning News* is a daily filled with information about local cultural and entertainment events. The *Savannah Tribune* and the *Herald of Savannah* are geared to the African-American community.

Post Offices   Post offices and sub-post offices are centrally located and open Monday to Friday 7am to 6pm and Saturday 9am to 3pm. The main office is at 2 N. Fahn St. (✆ **912/235-4653**).

Safety   Although it's reasonably safe to explore the Historic and Victorian districts during the day, the situation changes at night. The clubs along the riverfront, both bars and restaurants, report very little crime. However, muggings and drug dealing are common in the poorer neighborhoods of Savannah.

Taxes The city of Savannah adds a 2% local option tax to the 4% state tax.

Transit Information Call **Chatham Area Transit** at $\textcircled{C}$ **912/ 233-5767.**

Weather Call $\textcircled{C}$ **912/964-1700.**

3 Where to Stay

The undisputed stars here are the small inns in the Historic District, most in restored old homes that have been renovated with modern conveniences while retaining every bit of their original charm.

A note on rates: Because many of Savannah's historic inns are in converted former residences, price ranges can vary greatly. A very expensive hotel might also have some smaller and more moderately priced units. So it pays to ask. Advance reservations are necessary in most cases, since many of the best properties are quite small.

ALONG THE RIVERFRONT
EXPENSIVE

Hyatt Regency Savannah $\mathcal{R}\mathcal{R}$ There was an outcry from Savannah's historic preservation movement when this place went up in 1981. Boxy and massively bulky, it stands in unpleasant contrast to the restored warehouses flanking it along the legendary banks of the Savannah River. Today it is grudgingly accepted as the biggest and flashiest hotel in town. It has a soaring atrium as well as glass-sided elevators. The comfortable rooms are international and modern in their feel, all with good-size baths and many with balconies overlooking the atrium. Room prices vary according to their views—units without a view are quite a bargain. There's a stylish bar and two restaurants with a big-city feel and views over the river.

2 W. Bay St., Savannah, GA 31401. $\textcircled{C}$ **800/228-1234** or 912/238-1234. Fax 912/ 944-3678. www.hyatt.com. E-mail: tmunroe@savrspo.hyatt.com. 347 units. $150–$240 double; $234–$900 suite. AE, DC, DISC, MC, V. Parking $13. **Amenities:** 2 restaurants; bar; health club; indoor pool; small fitness room. *In room:* A/C, TV.

Ballastone Inn **14**

Bed & Breakfast Inn **18**

Catherine Ward House Inn **19**

Courtyard by Marriott **24**

DeSoto Hilton **16**

East Bay Inn **6**

Eliza Thompson House **17**

Fairfield Inn by Marriott **24**

Foley House Inn **15**

The Forsyth Park Inn **21**

Gaston Gallery Bed & Breakfast **25**

The Gastonian **26**

Granite Steps Inn **23**

Hampton Inn **4**

Hyatt Regency Savannah **2**

The Kehoe House **11**

Magnolia Place Inn **20**

Marshall House **10**

The Mulberry-Holiday Inn **9**

Olde Harbour Inn **7**

Park Avenue Manor **22**

Planters Inn **3**

The Presidents' Quarters **13**

River Street Inn **5**

Savannah Marriott Riverfront **8**

17 Hundred 90 **12**

Westin Savannah Harbor Resort **1**

Savannah Marriott Riverfront Hotel 🏕️   At least the massive modern bulk of this place is far enough from the 19th-century restored warehouses of River Street not to clash with them aesthetically. Towering eight stories, with an angular facade sheathed in orange and yellow brick, it doesn't quite succeed at being a top-rated luxury palace but nonetheless attracts lots of corporate business and conventions. We prefer the Hyatt, but this one can be a backup, with comfortable, modern rooms that aren't style-setters but are generous in space, with baths large enough to store your stuff and a generous supply of towels. The lobby restaurant, T.G.I. Fridays, suffers from a claustrophobically low ceiling and has faux-Victorian decor with a kaleidoscope of stained-glass lamps.

100 General McIntosh Blvd., Savannah, GA 31401. 🄫 **800/228-9290** or 912/233-7722. Fax 912/233-3765. www.marriott.com. E-mail: bssmith@savmarriott.com. 383 units. $149–$225 double; $195–$249 suite. Children 17 and under stay free in parents' room. AE, DC, DISC, MC, V. Parking $7. **Amenities:** Restaurant; dry cleaning/laundry service; secretarial services; indoor and outdoor pools; Jacuzzi; health club; business and conference rooms; tour desk; small boutique. *In room:* A/C, TV.

Westin Savannah Harbor Resort 🏕️   Savannah's largest hotel was opened late in 1999 in a 16-story blockbuster format that dwarfs the city's existing B&Bs. It rises somewhat jarringly from what were until the late 1990s sandy, scrub-covered flatlands on the swampy, rarely visited far side of the river from Savannah's historic core. Conceived as part of a massive resort development project, it derives the bulk of its business from corporate groups who arrive as part of large conventions throughout the year. It's the newest and largest of the four large-scale hotels that dominate the city's convention business, yet despite a worthy collection (more than 250 pieces) of contemporary art that accents the labyrinth of high-ceilinged public rooms here, there's something just a bit sterile, even lifeless, about this relatively anonymous blockbuster hotel. Compounding the problem is its isolated position, both geographically and emotionally, from the bustle, grace, and charm of central Savannah—this in spite of cross-river shuttle ferries that deposit clients into the center of the River Street bar and restaurant frenzy. The most elaborate bedrooms are on the two top floors, and contain extra amenities and comforts designated as Club Level. Otherwise, rooms are comfortable but bland, outfitted in pale colors and conservative furnishings.

There's an 18-hole golf course designed by Sam Snead and Bob Cupp, and the world's only branch of the Greenbriar (West

Virginia) Spa. Set within an ochre-colored annex, and outfitted with the leafy, pale green decor of its namesake, it offers hydrotherapy and massage sessions. On the premises are two not-particularly exciting restaurants, The Aqua Star, and its less pretentious sibling, The Grill, which lies in the Golf Course Clubhouse. Our favorite is the Midnight Sun Bar, a woodsy-looking bar based on a theme inspired by the musical career of local songwriter Johnny Mercer.

One Resort Drive, PO Box 427, Savannah, GA 31421. © 800/WESTIN-1 or 912/ 201-2000. Fax 912/201-2001. www.westinsavannah.com. 403 units. $219–$299 double, $275–$800 suite. Water taxis, free for hotel guests, $2 round-trip for everyone else, shuttle across the river to Rousakis Plaza, on River Street, at 15-minute intervals. From I-95 and Savannah International Airport: Take Exit 17A to I-16 toward Savannah. Follow sign for Rt. 17-Talmadge Bridge. Take Hutchinson Island Exit onto Resort Drive. **Amenities:** 2 restaurants; bar; 24-hr. room service; 4 Har-Tru tennis courts that are illuminated for night play; a 400-ft. floating dock for mooring yachts in the nearby river; 2 outdoor pools; 18-hole golf course; Greenbriar Spa. *In room:* A/C, TV, minibar.

MODERATE

Olde Harbour Inn *𝒢*   The neighborhood has been gentrified and the interior of this place is well furnished, but you still get a whiff of riverfront seediness as you approach from Factors Walk. It was built in 1892 as a warehouse for oil, and its masonry bulk is camouflaged with shutters, awnings, and touches of wrought iron. Inside, a labyrinth of passages leads to small but comfortable suites, many of which show the building's massive timbers and structural iron brackets and offer views of the river. Some decors feature the original brick, painted white. Each unit contains its own kitchen— useful for anyone in town for an extended stay. Despite the overlay of chintz, you'll have a constant sense of the building's thick-walled bulk. Breakfast is the only meal served.

508 E. Factors Walk, Savannah, GA 31401. © 800/553-6533 or 912/234-4100. Fax 912/233-5979. www.oldeharbourinn.com. 24 units. $149–$259 suite. Rates include continental breakfast. AE, DISC, DC, MC, V. *In room:* A/C, TV.

River Street Inn   When Liverpool-based ships were moored on the nearby river, this building stored massive amounts of cotton produced by upriver plantations. After the boll weevil decimated the cotton industry, it functioned as an icehouse, a storage area for fresh vegetables, and (at its lowest point) the headquarters of an insurance company. Its two lowest floors, built in 1817, were made of ballast stones carried in the holds of ships from faraway England.

In 1986, a group of investors poured millions into its development as one of the linchpins of Savannah's River District, adding a

Kids **Family-Friendly Hotels**

The Mulberry/Holiday Inn *(see p. 110)*   Right in the heart of the Historic District is a family hotel that lets kids under 18 stay free if sharing a room with their parents. Children enjoy the pool, and cribs are provided free.

Hampton Inn *(see p. 113)*   One of the most appealing of the city's middle-bracket hotels, this family favorite rises on historic Bay Street. Rooms are spacious, and there's a pool and sundeck on the roof.

River Street Inn *(see p. 105)*   The best bet for families with children along the riverfront is a converted cotton warehouse from 1817. Large rooms make family life easier, and children under 18 stay free. There's also a game room, and many fast-food joints are just outside the front door.

well-upholstered colonial pizzazz to the public areas and converting the building's warren of brick-lined storerooms into some of the most comfortable and well-managed rooms in town. There are many pluses to staying here, including the location, near loads of restaurants and nightclubs. Breakfast is served in Huey's (see "Where to Dine," later in this chapter). A wine-and-cheese reception is held Monday to Saturday, and turndown service is offered each evening.

115 E. River St., Savannah, GA 31401. *(*© **800/253-4229** or 912/234-6400. Fax 912/234-1478. www.riverstreetinn.com. E-mail: www.riverstreetinn@hotmail.com. @riverstreetinn.com. 86 units. $159–$275 double. AE, DC, MC, V. Parking $4. *In room:* A/C, TV.

IN THE HISTORIC DISTRICT
VERY EXPENSIVE

Ballastone Inn *☆☆*   This glamorous inner-city B&B occupies a dignified 1838 building separated from the Juliette Gordon Low House (original home of the founder of the Girl Scouts of America) by a well-tended formal garden; it's richly decorated with all the hardwoods, elaborate draperies, and antique furniture you'd expect. For a brief period (only long enough to add a hint of spiciness), the place functioned as a bordello *and* a branch office for the Girl Scouts (now next door).

There's an elevator, unusual for Savannah B&Bs, but no closets (they were taxed as extra rooms in the old days and so never added); there are many truly unusual furnishings—cachepots filled with scented potpourri, and art objects that would thrill the heart of any decorator. A full-service bar area is tucked into a corner of what was originally a double parlor. The four suites are in a clapboard townhouse a 5-minute walk away and staffed with its own live-in receptionists. A year-long refurbishment project in 1997 resulted in a four-diamond distinction.

Though the hotel doesn't serve lunch or dinner, many dining options are nearby. The recent hiring of a chef, however, vastly improved the quality of the breakfast, and the chef also prepares the afternoon tea and evening hors d'oeuvres.

14 E. Oglethorpe Ave., Savannah, GA 31401. ℂ **800/822-4553** or 912/236-1484. Fax 912/236-4626. 16 units. $250–$375 double; $375–$420 suite. Rates include full breakfast, afternoon tea, and evening hors d'oeuvres. AE, MC, V. Free parking. No children. **Amenities:** 24-hr. concierge; laundry; nearby health club with free weights and pool; twice-daily maid service with turndown. *In room:* A/C, TV.

The Gastonian 𝒜𝒜   One of the two or three posh B&Bs in Savannah, the Gastonian incorporates a pair of Italianate Regency buildings constructed in 1868 by the same unknown architect. Hard times began with the 1929 stock market crash—the buildings were divided into apartments for the payment of back taxes. In 1984, the Lineberger family visiting from California saw the place, fell in love with it, and poured $2 million into restoring it. Today everything is a testimonial to Victorian charm, except for a skillfully crafted serpentine bridge connecting the two buildings and curving above a verdant semitropical garden. The rooms are appropriately plush, comfortable, cozy, and beautifully furnished.

Afternoon tea is served in a formal English-inspired drawing room where Persian carpets and a grand piano add to the luster of the good life from another era; a full breakfast is offered in the dining room with seatings at 8 and 10am.

220 E. Gaston St., Savannah, GA 31401. ℂ **800/322-6603** or 912/232-2869. Fax 912/232-0710. www.gastonian.com. E-mail: gastonian@aol.com. 17 units. $225–$295 double; from 375 suite. Rates include full breakfast. AE, DISC, MC, V. No children under 12. **Amenities:** Concierge; tour desk; courtyard and deck with hot tub; meeting rooms. *In room:* A/C, TV.

Granite Steps Inn 𝒜   This inn is glossier, larger, more opulent, and contains fewer accommodations than most of its other competitors in Savannah. Originally built in 1881 as a showy Italianate residence for a successful cotton merchant, it later belonged to celebrity decorator Jim Williams (the alleged murderer of Danny Hansford in The Book) just before his death. In May 1998, it was lavishly restored by a team of hardworking entrepreneurs associated with Georgia's premier spa, the Chateau Elan, outside Atlanta. Consequently, you'll find more emphasis on hot tubs (most rooms contain one) and somewhat fussy pampering than at any other B&B in town. None of this is lost on such clients as Hollywood producer Nora Ephron (*Sleepless in Seattle; You've Got Mail*) and other West Coast customers who appreciate the inn's striking mixture of Gilded Age glamour, gilded Japanese screens, and free-form modern art decorating the public areas. The midsize-to-spacious bedrooms are endlessly tasteful and very upscale. If you decide to stay here, don't expect down-home Southern folksiness, as the setting is simply too urbane, too discreet, too restrained, and too linked to the European spa motif for hush-puppy, cornpone regionalisms to surface, let alone survive.

126 E. Gaston St., Savannah, GA 31401. (© 912/233-5380. Fax 912/236-3116. www.granitesteps.com. 5 units. $275 double; $375 suite. AE, MC, V. *In room:* A/C, TV.

The Kehoe House 🕸🕸🕸   The Kehoe was built in 1892. In the 1950s, after the place had been converted into a funeral parlor, its owners tried to tear down the nearby Davenport House (see "Seeing the Sights," later in this chapter) to build a parking lot. The resulting outrage led to the founding of the Historic Savannah Association and the salvation of most of the neighborhood's remaining historic buildings.

Today, the place functions as a spectacularly opulent B&B, with a collection of fabrics and furniture that's almost forbiddingly valuable. However, it lacks the warmth and welcome of the Ballastone. This isn't a place for children—the ideal guest will tread softly on floors that are considered models of historic authenticity and flawless taste. Breakfast and afternoon tea are part of the ritual that has seduced such former clients as Tom Hanks, who stayed in room 301 during the filming of parts of *Forrest Gump.* The rooms are spacious, with the typical 12-foot ceilings, and each is tastefully furnished in English period antiques. Owners Rob and Jane Sales and Kathy Medlock acquired it in 1997 and immediately renovated the back garden, in addition to expanding the guest parking area. Amenities include a concierge and twice-daily maid service with turndown.

123 Habersham St., Savannah, GA 31401. (© 800/820-1020 or 912/232-1020. Fax 912/231-0208. www.kehoehouse.com. 15 units. $205–$245 double; $275 suite. Rates include full breakfast. AE, DC, DISC, MC, V. *In room:* A/C, TV.

Magnolia Place Inn 🏰 This building was begun in 1878 on a desirable plot overlooking Forsyth Square and completed 4 years later by a venerable family who'd been forced off their upriver plantation after the Civil War for nonpayment of taxes. An ancestor had represented South Carolina at the signing of the Declaration of Independence, and so the Second Empire ("steamboat Gothic") house was designed to be as grand as funds would allow. The result includes the most endearing front steps in town (Neiman Marcus asked to display them as a backdrop for one of its catalogs but the negotiations broke down), verandas worthy of a Mississippi steamer, and an oval skylight (an "oculus") that illuminates a graceful staircase ascending to the dignified rooms. Amenities include a 24-hr. concierge, a tour desk, meeting spaces, access to a nearby health club, and bicycle rentals.

503 Whitaker St., Savannah, GA 31401. ⓒ 800/238-7674 outside Georgia, or 912/236-7674. Fax 912/236-1145. www.magnoliaplaceinn.com. E-mail: info@magnoliaplaceinn.com. 13 units. $145–$270 double. Rates include full breakfast, afternoon tea, and evening hors d'oeuvres. AE, DC, DISC, MC, V. Free parking. *In room:* A/C, TV.

EXPENSIVE

Catherine Ward House Inn 🏰 The restoration of this house has won several civic awards, and it's so evocative of Savannah's "carpenter Gothic" Victorian revival that Clint Eastwood inserted a long, graceful shot of its exterior in *Midnight in the Garden of Good and Evil*. Built by a sea captain for his wife (Catherine Ward) in 1886 in a location a short walk from Forsyth Park, it offers one of the most lavishly decorated interiors of any B&B in Savannah, but at prices that are significantly less than those offered at better-known B&Bs a few blocks away. Alan Williams, the owner and innkeeper, maintains a policy that discourages children under 16, and that stresses a gay-friendly but even-handed approach to a widely diverse clientele. Breakfast is relatively elaborate, served on fine porcelain in a grandly outfitted dining room. A garden in back encourages languid sun-dappled dialogues. Each midsize bedroom is individually and richly decorated.

118 East Waldburg St., Savannah, GA 31401. ⓒ 912/234-8564. Fax 912/231-8007. www.catherinewardhouseinn.com. 10 units. $129–$300 double. DISC, MC, V. *In room:* A/C, TV.

DeSoto Hilton 🏰 The name still evokes a bit of glamour—built in 1890, this hotel was for many generations the city's grandest. In 1967, thousands of wedding receptions, Kiwanis meetings, and debutante parties later, the building was demolished and rebuilt in a bland modern format. It's a well-managed commercial hotel, fully renovated by new owners in 1995. The rooms are conservatively modern and reached after registering in a stone-sheathed lobby whose decor was partly inspired by an 18th-century colonial drawing room. Despite the absence of antique charm, many guests like this place for its polite efficiency and modernism.

In the late 1990s, the inn was acquired by one of Georgia's most dedicated and successful innkeepers, Phil Jenkins, a noted musicologist and conductor who was responsible for the revitalization of a historic landmark (the 1842 Inn) in Macon. Emphasizing his new inn's colonial coastal theme, and adding sophisticated touches of *trompe l'oeil* to hallways and salons, he presents a unique afternoon experience every day between 5:30 and 7pm. Then, garnished with glasses of wine and platters of fruit and cheese, Phil or any of his (highly talented) employees will sing and play the piano or guitar as part of a genteel roster of mid-afternoon entertainment. On the premises is the Lion's Den bar (formerly a famous club known as Mercers), a coffee shop (Knickerbocker's), and a more formal restaurant, the Pavillion. Children under 12 are discouraged.

15 E. Liberty St. (P.O. Box 8207), Savannah, GA 31412. ✆ 800/445-8667 or 912/232-9000. Fax 921/232-6018. www.hilton.com. 246 units. $79–$239 double. AE, DC, MC, V. **Amenities:** Restaurant; coffee shop; bar; concierge; laundry/dry cleaning; pool deck; fitness center with access to the Downtown Athletic Club; golf privileges. *In room:* A/C, TV.

Foley House Inn 🏵 Decorated with all the care of a private home, this small B&B occupies a brick-sided house built in 1896. Its owners doubled its size by acquiring the simpler white-fronted house next door, whose pedigree predates its neighbors by half a century. The staff will regale you with tales of the original residents of both houses—one was the site of a notorious turn-of-the-century suicide. Breakfast and afternoon hors d'oeuvres, tea, and cordials are served in a large, verdant space formed by the two houses' connected gardens.

14 W. Hull St., Savannah, GA 31401. ✆ 800/647-3708 or 912/232-6622. Fax 912/231-1218. www.foleyinn.com. E-mail: foleyinn@aol.com. 19 units. $185–$290 double. Rates include full breakfast, afternoon hors d'oeuvres, tea, and cordials. AE, DC, MC, V. No children under 12. **Amenities:** Concierge; laundry/dry cleaning. *In room:* A/C, TV.

The Mulberry/Holiday Inn 🏵 Locals point with pride to the Mulberry as a sophisticated adaptation of what might've been a derelict building into a surprisingly elegant hotel. Built in 1868 as a stable and cotton warehouse, it was converted in 1982 into a simple hotel, and in the 1990s it received a radical upgrade and a dash of decorator-inspired Chippendale glamour. Today, its lobby looks like that of a grand hotel in London, and the rooms, though small, have a formal decor (think English country-house look with a Southern accent). The hotel's brick-covered patio, with fountains, trailing ivy, and wrought-iron furniture, evokes the best aspects of New Orleans. On the premises are a bar, Sergeant Jasper's Lounge, and two restaurants, the Cafe for breakfast and dinner and the Mulberry for more formal dinners.

601 E. Bay St., Savannah, GA 31401. ℂ **800/465-4329** or 912/238-1200. Fax 912/236-2184. www.savannahhotel.com. E-mail: jrettberg@princebush.com. 145 units. $179–$249 double; $229 suite. Children under 18 stay free in parents' room. AE, DC, DISC, MC, V. Parking $5. **Amenities:** Restaurant; pool; sundeck; Jacuzzi; access to nearby health club. *In room:* A/C, TV.

The Presidents' Quarters 🔾   This hotel has many appealing aspects. The rooms and baths are among the largest and most comfortable of any inn in Savannah. It manages simultaneously to combine the charm of a B&B with the efficiency of a much larger place. It has appealed to guests as diverse as the former president of Ireland and numbers of Hollywood actors. Each accommodation is named after a U.S. president who visited Savannah during his term in office. A continental breakfast and afternoon tea are served each day on the brick patio off the back of the house.

255 E. President St., Savannah, GA 31401. ℂ **800/233-1776** or 912/233-1600. Fax 912/238-0849. www.presidentsquarters.com. E-mail: pqinn@aol.com. 19 units. $147–$235 double. Rates include breakfast. DC, DISC, MC, V. Free parking on premises. **Amenities:** Room service; outdoor whirlpool/Jacuzzi; conference rooms; dry cleaning; access to a nearby health club. *In room:* A/C, TV.

MODERATE

East Bay Inn   Though the views from its windows might be uninspired, the East Bay is conveniently located near the bars and attractions of the riverfront. It was built in 1853 as a cotton warehouse; green awnings and potted geraniums disguise the building's once-utilitarian design. A cozy lobby contains Chippendale furnishings and elaborate moldings. The rooms have queen-size four-poster beds, reproductions of antiques, and coffeemakers. The hotel frequently houses tour groups from Europe and South America. In the cellar is **Skyler's** (ℂ **912/232-3955**), an independently managed restaurant specializing in European and Asian cuisine.

225 E. Bay St., Savannah, GA 31401. ℂ **800/500-1225** or 912/238-1225. Fax 912/232-2709. www.eastbayinn.com. 28 units. $159–$210 double. AE, DC, MC, V. *In room:* A/C, TV.

Eliza Thompson House ☆☆   The rooms of this stately home are equally divided between the original 1847 building and a converted carriage house. Both were the domain of Eliza Thompson, a socially conscious matriarch whose husband (a cotton merchant) died shortly after the foundations were laid. After serving as a shop for antiques dealers, it was bought by new owners in 1997. Steve and Carol Day have completely redecorated, using original Savannah colors, beautiful antiques, and Oriental carpets. The heart pine floors have been restored to their original luster, the linens have been replaced, and a program of ironing each sheet and pillowcase has begun. The inn now provides comfortable cotton robes in each room and a turndown service. It's also graced with one of the most beautiful courtyards in the city, featuring three large fountains, sago palms, and camellias. The rooms are comfortable, elegant, and cozy, furnished with tradition and taste. Breakfast is usually a lavish affair, featuring sausage casserole, muffins, and croissants. During nice weather, it's usually served on the brick terrace of the garden patio separating the two components of this historic inn.

5 W. Jones St., Savannah, GA 31401. ✆ **800/348-9378** or 912/236-3620. Fax 912/238-1920. www.elizathompsonhouse.com. 25 units. $109–$260 double. Rates include continental breakfast. AE, MC, V. *In room:* A/C, TV.

The Forsyth Park Inn   One of the grandest houses on the western flank of Forsyth Park is this yellow frame place built in the 1890s by a sea captain (Aaron Flynt, a.k.a. Rudder Churchill). A richly detailed staircase winds upstairs from a paneled vestibule, and the Queen Anne decor of the formal robin's-egg-blue salon extends through the rest of the house. Guest rooms have oak paneling and oversize doors that are testimonials to turn-of-the-century craftsmanship. The more expensive rooms, including one in what used to be the dining room, are among the largest in town. Home-baked breads and pastries are a staple of the breakfasts. Don't expect frivolity: The inn is just a bit staid.

102 W. Hall St., Savannah, GA 31401. ✆ **912/233-6800.** Fax 912/233-6804. www.forsythparkinn.com. 9 units, 1 cottage with kitchenette. $115–$230 double; $220 cottage. AE, DISC, MC, V. *In room:* A/C, TV.

Gaston Gallery Bed & Breakfast   This major investment in period restoration was built as two separate houses united by a shared Italianate facade. In 1997, a lavish reunification of the two houses was undertaken. Today, the unified building bears the distinction of having the city's longest and most stately front porch (called a gallery in Savannah) and inner ceilings that are almost dizzyingly high. The breakfasts are social events, each featuring a different dish, like curried eggs or Southern grits casserole. Wine and cheese are served every day at 5pm or on your arrival, according to your wishes.

211 E. Gaston St., Savannah, GA 31401. © **800/671-0716** or 912/238-3294. Fax 912/238-4064. www.gastongallery.com. 15 units. $90–$200 double. AE, DISC, MC, V. *In room:* TV.

Hampton Inn   This is the most appealing of the city's middle-bracket large-scale hotels. Opened in 1997, it rises seven redbrick stories above the busy traffic of historic Bay Street, across from Savannah's Riverwalk and some of the city's most animated nightclubs. Its big-windowed lobby was designed to mimic an 18th-century Savannah salon, thanks to the recycling of heart pine flooring from an old sawmill in central Georgia and the use of antique Savannah bricks. Comfortably formal seating arrangements, a blazing fireplace, and an antique bar add cozy touches. The rooms are simple and comfortable, with wall-to-wall carpeting, medium-size tile baths, and flowered upholstery. On the roof is a small pool and sundeck that's supplemented with an exercise room on the seventh floor. There's no restaurant, but many eateries are a short walk away.

201 E. Bay St., Savannah, GA. © **800/426-7866** or 912/232-9700. Fax 912/231-0440. www.hampton-inn.com. 144 units. Sun–Thurs $129–$159 double; Fr–Sat $139–$169 double. AE, DC, MC, V. Parking $5. *In room:* A/C, TV.

Marshall House   Some aspects of this hotel—especially the second-story cast-iron veranda that juts out above the sidewalk—might remind you of a 19th-century hotel in the French Quarter of New Orleans. It originally opened in 1851 as the then-finest hotel in Savannah. In 1864-65, it functioned as a Union Army hospital, before housing such luminaries as Conrad Aiken and Joel Chandler Harris, author of *Stories of Uncle Remus.* After a ratty-looking decline, it closed—some people thought permanently—in 1957. In 1999, it reopened as a "boutique-style" inn. Despite the fact that this place has some of the trappings of an upscale B&B, don't think that it will provide the intimacy or exclusivity of, say, the Foley House. There's something a bit superficial about the glamour here, and some aspects evoke a busy motel, albeit with a more than usual elegant set of colonial-era reproductions in the public areas. Bedrooms succeed at being mass-production-style cozy without being particularly opulent; each sheathed in one of three standardized possibilities: yellow with pinewood furniture, green with wrought-iron furniture, and blue with white-painted furniture.

Seven of the largest and most historically evocative rooms in the hotel are on the second floor, overlooking noisy Broughton Street, and are prefaced with wrought-iron verandas with wrought-iron furniture. Room service is daily from 6am to 11pm. Chadwick's is a bar with exposed brick, a very Southern clientele, green leather upholstery, and occasional presentations of live jazz. The Café M, set beneath the glassed-in roof of what used to be the hotel's rear stable yard, is a restaurant serving Southern and international cuisine.

123 E. Broughton St., Savannah, GA 31401. © **800/589-6304** or 912/644-7896. www.marshallhouse.com. 68 units. $99–$199 double; $225–$350 suite. AE, MC, V. *In room:* A/C, TV, minibar.

Park Avenue Manor   Historic and cozy, this is Savannah's premier gay-friendly guesthouse. An 1897 Victorian B&B, it has an old-fashioned charm with antiques, double staircases, two formal parlors, and angel ceiling borders. Many accommodations have four-poster beds with antiques, silk carpets, porcelains, working fireplaces, and period prints. The small-scale inn has a well-rehearsed management style and an emphasis on irreverently offbeat Savannah. Many straight clients also book here, as the place is noted not only for its comfort but its warm welcome and one of the best Southern breakfasts served in town. The guesthouse was created in 1997, when a pair of Victorian houses were "sewn" together into a tasteful whole. A favorite is the Robert E. Lee room with a large bay window.

107–109 W. Park Ave., Savannah, GA 31402. © **912/233-0352.** www.bbonline. com/ga/parkavenue. E-mail: pkavemanor@aol.com. 5 units. $95–$165 double; $170 suite. AE, MC, V.

Planters Inn   This small European-style inn is more businesslike than the average Savannah B&B. Built adjacent to Reynolds Square in 1912 as a seven-story brown brick tower, it boasts a lobby with elaborate millwork, a scattering of Chippendale reproductions, and an honor bar (sign for whatever drink you consume). The rooms are comfortably outfitted with four-poster beds and flowery fabrics; they're rather dignified and formal. The Planters Inn isn't associated with the well-recommended Planters Tavern (which stands next door and is separate).

29 Abercorn St., Savannah, GA 31401. © **800/554-1187** or 912/232-5678. Fax 912/232-8893. www.plantersinnsavannah.com. E-mail: plantinn@aol.com. 59 units. $125–$165 double. Rates include continental breakfast. AE, DC, MC, V. Parking $6.75. *In room:* A/C, TV.

17 Hundred 90 *𝒢* A severely dignified brick-and-clapboard structure, this place will remind you of New England's low-ceilinged 18th-century houses. It's the oldest inn in Savannah, permeated with conversation and laughter from the basement-level bar and restaurant (see "Where to Dine," below), and by the spirits of its resident ghosts. The most famous is the daughter of the building's first owner, young Anna, who hurled herself over the balcony to her death on the brick walk below as her sailor love sailed away. Accessible via cramped hallways, the rooms are small yet charming, outfitted with the colonial trappings appropriate for an inn of this age and stature. About a dozen contain fireplaces and small refrigerators.

307 E. President St., Savannah, GA 31401. *©* **800/487-1790** or 912/236-7122. Fax 912/236-7123. www.17hundred90.com. E-mail: 1790inn@msn.com. 14 units. $119–$189 double. AE, MC, V. *In room:* A/C, TV.

INEXPENSIVE

Bed and Breakfast Inn Adjacent to Chatham Square, in the oldest part of historic Savannah, this is a dignified stone-fronted townhouse built in 1853. You climb a gracefully curved front stoop to reach the cool high-ceilinged interior, outfitted with a combination of antique and reproduction furniture. Some of the good-size comfortable and tastefully furnished accommodations contain refrigerators. There's no smoking.

117 W. Gordon St. (at Chatham Sq.), Savannah, GA 31401. *©* **912/238-0518.** Fax 912/233-2537. www.travelbase.com/destinations/savannah/bed-breakfast. E-mail: bnbinn@msn.com. 18 units. $79–$150 double. Rates include full breakfast. AE, DISC, MC, V. *In room:* A/C, TV.

Courtyard by Marriott Built around a landscaped courtyard, this is one of the more recommendable motels bordering the Historic District. Many Savannah motels, though cheap, are quite tacky, but this one has renovated rooms with separate seating areas, oversized desks, and private patios or balconies. Family-friendly, the hotel offers a coin laundry, free cribs, and both a pool and a whirlpool. The restaurant serves a la carte and buffet breakfasts. Exercise equipment includes weights and bicycles.

6703 Abercorn St., Savannah, GA 31405. *©* **800/321-2211** or 912/354-7878. Fax 912/352-1432. www.marriott.com. 144 units. $75–$102 double; from $119–$129 suite. Children 15 and under stay free in parents' room. Senior discounts available. AE, DC, DISC, MC, V. Parking $2.50. From I-16, take Exit 34A to I-516 East and turn right on Abercorn St. *In room:* A/C, TV.

Fairfield Inn by Marriott   Not quite as good as Marriott's other recommended motel (above), this reliable budget hotel offers standard but comfortably appointed rooms, with in-room movies and a large, well-lit desk. The big attraction here is an outdoor pool. Health-club privileges are available nearby, as are several good moderately priced restaurants.

2 Lee Blvd. (at Abercorn Rd.), Savannah, GA 31405. ℂ **800/228-2800** or 912/353-7100. Fax 912/353-7100. www.marriott.com. 135 units. $54–$70 double. Children 17 and under stay free in parents' room. AE, DC, DISC, MC, V. Free parking. From I-16, take Exit 34A to I-516 East, then turn right on Abercorn St. and go right again on Lee Blvd. *In room:* A/C, TV.

4 Where to Dine

Savannah is known for the excellence of its seafood restaurants. They're among the best in Georgia, rivaled only by those in Atlanta. The best dining is in the Historic District, along River Street, bordering the water. However, locals also like to escape the city and head for the seafood places on Tybee and other offshore islands.

Some of Savannah's restaurants, like Elizabeth on 37th, are ranked among the finest in the entire South. And others, like Mrs. Wilkes' Dining Room, are places to go for real Southern fare—from collard greens and fried okra to fried chicken, cornbread, and hot biscuits.

ALONG OR NEAR THE WATERFRONT
EXPENSIVE

The Chart House   ℱ   STEAK/SEAFOOD   Overlooking the Savannah River and Riverfront Plaza, "the home of the mud pie" is part of a nationwide chain—and one of the better ones. It's housed in a building that predates 1790, reputed to be the oldest masonry structure in Georgia and once a sugar-and-cotton warehouse. You can enjoy a view of passing ships on the outside deck, perhaps even order an appetizer and a drink before dinner. The bar is one of the most atmospheric along the riverfront. As in all Chart Houses, the prime rib is slow-roasted and served au jus. The steaks from corn-fed beef are aged and hand-cut on the premises before being charcoal-grilled. The most expensive item is lobster. You may prefer one of the fresh catches of the day, which can be grilled to your specifications.

202 W. Bay St. ℂ **912/234-6686.** Reservations recommended. Main courses $14.95–$23.95. AE, DC, DISC, MC, V. Mon–Fri 5–10pm, Sat 5–10:30pm, Sun 5–9pm.

Billy Bob's **15**
The Chart House **14**
Clary's Café **4**
Elizabeth on 37th **3**
The Exchange Tavern **19**
45 South **20**
Garibaldi's **11**
Huey's **17**
Il Pasticcio **9**
Johnny Harris Restaurant **2**

Lady and Sons **13**
Mrs. Wilkes' Boarding House **5**
Nita's Place **6**
The Olde Pink House Restaurant **16**
The River's End **1**
Sapphire Grill **10**
17 Hundred 90 **8**
Shrimp Factory **18**
606 East Café **12**
Wall's **7**

MODERATE

Huey's 🦀 CAJUN/CREOLE   At first glance, this casual place overlooking the Savannah River seems little different from the other restored warehouses. But you'll discover it's special when you taste the food, created under the direction of Louisiana-born Mike Jones. He even manages to please visitors from New Orleans—and that's saying a lot. The place is often packed. Breakfast begins with such dishes as a Creole omelet, followed by an oyster "Po' Boy" for lunch. It's at dinner, however, that the kitchen really shines, producing jambalaya with andouille sausage, crayfish étouffée, and crab-and-shrimp au gratin (with Louisiana crabmeat and Georgia shrimp). The soups are homemade and the appetizers distinctive. A jazz brunch is featured Saturday and Sunday 8am to 3pm. The bar next door offers live entertainment.

In the River Street Inn, 115 E. River St. © 912/234-7385. Reservations recommended. Main courses $9.95–$20; sandwiches $6–$10. AE, DISC, MC, V. Mon–Thurs 7am–10pm, Fri–Sat 7am–11pm, Sun 8am–10pm.

INEXPENSIVE

Billy Bob's BARBECUE/SEAFOOD   Its decor was modeled after a barn somewhere on the panhandle of Texas; the recorded music might remind you of the country-western tunes they play at this place's namesake in Houston. The barbecues here are succulent and tender, having been slowly marinated and spicily flavored. Examples are baby-back ribs, barbecued chicken, shrimp, and beef-steaks. Appetizers feature a warm crab-and-artichoke dip and oysters Rockefeller, and steaks and seafood include grilled swordfish, battered shrimp platters, and at least five kinds of Angus beef.

21 E. River St. © **912/234-5588.** Reservations not necessary. Main courses $5.95–$21.95. AE, DISC, MC, V. Sun–Thurs 11am–10pm, Fri–Sat 11am–11pm.

The Exchange Tavern SEAFOOD/LOW COUNTRY   A local favorite, it's in a 1790s former cotton warehouse that opens onto the riverfront. The chefs make no pretense about their food. Everything is hale and hearty rather than gourmet. Your best bet is the ocean-fresh seafood, served grilled, broiled, or fried. Hand-cut grilled rib-eye steaks are a specialty, along with Buffalo-style wings, shrimp, oysters, and well-stuffed sandwiches served throughout the day. Since 1971, this place has been dispensing its wares, including shish kebabs, fresh salads, and homemade soups. It's also a good place for a drink.

201 E. River St. (east of Bull St.). © **912/232-7088.** Main courses $8.95–$18.95; child's plate $3.99. AE, DC, MC, V. Sun–Thurs 11am–11pm, Fri–Sat 11am–midnight.

Lady and Sons 𝖆𝖆 SOUTHERN   Paula Deen started this place in 1989 with $200, the help of her sons, and a 1910 structure. Today she runs one of Savannah's most celebrated restaurants. Her first cookbook, *Lady and Sons Savannah Country Cookbook* (Random House), is in its second printing (John Berendt wrote the introduction), and her second, *Lady and Sons Too,* was published in 2000. One taste of the food and you'll understand the roots of her success. Menu items like crab cakes (one Maryland visitor claimed they were the best he'd ever eaten), crab burgers, and several creative varieties of shrimp best exhibit her style. The locals love her buffets, which are very Southern. With fried chicken, meat loaf, collard greens, beef stew, "creamed" potatoes, or macaroni and cheese, this buffet is more aptly described as "more-than-you-can-eat."

Lunches are busy with a loyal following; dinners are casual and inventive. The aphrodisiac dish has to be the oyster shooters—half a dozen raw oysters, each served in a shot glass ("it's like killing two birds with one stone"). Paula's signature dish, chicken pot pie topped with puff pastry, looks so attractive you'll have reservations about eating it: Maybe that's why *Southern Living* used a picture of it in their magazine. Be careful not to fill up on the cheese biscuits and hoecakes that constantly land on your table. If for some reason you don't want a glorious glass of syrup-sweet tea, you'd better ask for unsweetened. But why rob yourself of the complete experience?

311 W. Congress St. ✆ **912/233-2600.** Reservations recommended for dinner. Main courses $6–$10 at lunch, $12–$20 at dinner; all-you-can-eat buffet $9.99 at lunch, $14.99 at dinner; $12.99 Sun lunch. AE, DISC, MC, V. Mon–Sat 11:30am–3pm; Mon–Thurs 5–9pm, Fri–Sat 5–10pm, Sun 11am–5pm.

Shrimp Factory SEAFOOD   The exposed old brick and wooden plank floors form a setting for harborside dining in a circa-1850 cotton warehouse. Lots of folks drop in before dinner to watch the boats pass by, perhaps enjoying a Chatham Artillery punch in a souvenir snifter. Yes, the place is touristy, never more so than when it welcomes tour buses. A salad bar rests next to a miniature shrimp boat, and fresh seafood comes from local waters. A specialty, pine bark stew, is served in a little iron pot with a bottle of sherry on the side; it's a potage of five kinds of seafood simmered with fresh herbs but minus the pine bark. Other dishes include peeled shrimp, shucked oysters, live Maine lobsters, sirloin steaks, and various fish filets.

313 E. River St. (2 blocks east of the Hyatt). ✆ **912/236-4229.** Reservations not accepted. Main courses $7.95–$14.95 at lunch, $10.50–$27.95 at dinner. AE, MC, V. Mon–Thurs 11am–10pm, Fri–Sat 11am–11pm, Sun noon–10pm.

IN THE HISTORIC DISTRICT
VERY EXPENSIVE

45 South ⍟⍟ INTERNATIONAL   Recommended by such magazines as *Food & Wine, Southern Living,* and even *Playboy,* this ritzy restaurant stands next door to the much more famous Pirates' House. The food has been called "gourmet Southern," and an ever-changing menu is likely to feature smoked North Carolina trout, rack of lamb flavored with crushed sesame seeds, grilled venison with au gratin of sweet potatoes, chicken breast with truffled paté, or sliced breast of pheasant with foie gras. Appetizers might include everything from South Carolina quail to crab cakes. Among the most expensive restaurants in Savannah, it's softly lit with elegantly set tables and a cozy bar. The service is impeccable.

20 E. Broad St. ℂ **912/233-1881.** Reservations suggested. Jackets advised. Main courses $21.50–$31.50. AE, MC, V. Mon–Thurs 6–9pm, Fri–Sat 6–9:30pm.

Sapphire Grill ⍟ AMERICAN/LOW COUNTRY   One of the city's most consistently stylish restaurants evokes a low-key, counter-culture bistro, but its cuisine is grander and more cutting-edge than its industrial-looking decor and its level of hipness would imply. Christopher Nason is the owner and the most talked-about chef of the moment in Savannah, preparing what he defines as a "coastal cuisine" based on seafood hauled in, usually on the day of its prepa-ration, from nearby waters. If you opt for a table here, you won't be alone: Scads of media and cinematic personalities will have preceded you. Collectively, they add an urban gloss of the type you might expect to see in Los Angeles. Launch your repast with a "firecracker salad"—that is, roasted red peppers and a red chili and shallot vinai-grette—or crisp fried green tomatoes, perhaps tuna medallions, and even James Island littleneck clams tossed in a foie gras butter, each beginning course a delectable choice. The chef is justifiably proud of such signature dishes as duck served with a roasted tomato cannel-loni or grilled prime tenderloin of beef with Dauphinoise potatoes. The local black grouper is flavored with lemon coriander, and a double-cut pork loin chop is one of the most elegant versions of this dish in Savannah. Each day the chef serves a tasting menu—based on the market price—that includes an appetizer, salad, main course, and confections. Ask about it, as it might be your best dining bet.

110 West Congress St. ℂ **912/443-9962.** Reservations recommended. Main courses $19–$34. AE, DC, MC, V. Sun–Thurs 6–10:30pm, Fri–Sat 5:30–11:30pm.

EXPENSIVE

The Olde Pink House Restaurant ✿✿ SEAFOOD/ AMERICAN   Built in 1771 and glowing pink (its antique bricks show through a protective covering of stucco), this house has functioned as a private home, a bank, a tearoom, and headquarters for one of Sherman's generals. Today, its interior is severe and dignified, with stiff-backed chairs, bare wooden floors, and an 18th-century aura similar to what you'd find in Williamsburg, Virginia. The cuisine is richly steeped in the traditions of the Low Country and includes crispy scored flounder with apricot sauce, steak au poivre, black grouper stuffed with blue crab and drenched in Vidalia onion sauce, and grilled tenderloin of pork crusted with almonds and molasses. You can enjoy your meal in the candlelit dining rooms or in the Planters Tavern.

23 Abercorn St. ✆ **912/232-4286.** Reservations recommended. Main courses $14.95–$24.95. AE, MC, V. Sun–Thurs 6–10:30pm, Fri–Sat 5:30–11pm.

17 Hundred 90 ✿ INTERNATIONAL   In the brick-lined cellar of Savannah's oldest inn (see "Where to Stay," earlier in this chapter), this place evokes a seafaring tavern along the coast of New England. Many visitors opt for a drink at the woodsy-looking bar in a separate back room before heading down the slightly claustrophobic corridor to the nautically inspired dining room. Students of paranormal psychology remain alert to the ghost rumored to wander through this place, site of Savannah's most famous 18th-century suicide. Lunch might include the quiche of the day with salad, Southern-style blue crab cakes, and a choice of salads and sandwiches. Dinners are more formal, featuring crab bisque, snapper Parmesan, steaks, and bourbon-flavored chicken. The cooking is of a high standard.

307 E. President St. ✆ **912/236-7122.** Reservations recommended. Main courses $17.95–$24.75. AE, MC, V. Mon–Fri noon–2pm and 6–10pm, Sat–Sun 6–10pm.

MODERATE

Il Pasticcio ITALIAN   This restaurant/bakery/gourmet market is one of the city's most popular dining spots. In a postmodern style, with big windows and a high ceiling, it has a definite big-city style. A rotisserie turns out specialties. Many locals come here just for the pasta dishes, all homemade and served with savory sauces. Begin with carpaccio (thinly sliced beef tenderloin) or a tricolor salad of radicchio, endive, and arugula. Main dishes are likely to feature a mixed grilled seafood platter or grilled fish steak with tricolor roasted sweet peppers.

2 E. Broughton St. (corner of Bull and Broughton sts.). © **912/231-8888**. Main courses $12.95–$22.95. AE, DC, V. Daily 5:30–10pm.

INEXPENSIVE

Clary's Café AMERICAN   Clary's Café has been a Savannah tradition since 1903, though the ambience today, under the devilish direction of Michael Faber, is decidedly 1950s. The place was famous long before it was featured in *Midnight in the Garden of Good and Evil* in its former role as Clary's drugstore, where regulars like eccentric flea-collar inventor Luther Driggers breakfasted and lunched. John Berendt is still a frequent patron, as is the fabled Lady Chablis. Begin your day with the classic Hoppel Poppel (scrambled eggs with chunks of kosher salami, potatoes, onions, and green peppers) and go on from there. Fresh salads, New York–style sandwiches, and stir-fries, along with grandmother's homemade chicken soup and flame-broiled burgers, are served throughout the day, giving way in the evening to chicken pot pie, stuffed pork loin, or planked fish (a fresh filet of red snapper—broiled, grilled, or blackened).

404 Abercorn St. (at Jones St.). © **912/233-0402**. Breakfast $4.50–$7.95; main courses $6.95–$10.95. AE, DC, DISC, MC, V. Mon–Fri 7am–4pm, Sat 8am–4:30pm, Sun 8am–4pm.

Mrs. Wilkes' Boarding House SOUTHERN   Remember the days of the boardinghouse, when everybody sat together, and belly-busting food was served in big dishes in the center of the table? Mrs. Selma Wilkes has been serving locals and travelers in just that manner since the 1940s. Bruce Willis and Demi Moore and Clint Eastwood are among the long list of celebrities who've dined here. Expect to find a long line of people patiently waiting for a seat at one of the long tables in the basement dining room of this 1870 brick house with curving steps and cast-iron trim.

Mrs. Wilkes believes in freshness and plans her daily menu around the seasons. Your food will be a reflection of the cuisine Savannah residents have enjoyed for generations—fried or barbecued chicken, red rice and sausage, black-eyed peas, corn on the cob, squash and yams, okra, cornbread, and collard greens.

107 W. Jones St. (west of Bull St.). © **912/232-5997**. Reservations not accepted. Breakfast $6; lunch $12. No credit cards. Mon–Fri 8–9am and 11:30am–3pm.

Nita's Place SOUTHERN   Nita's is a local institution favored by a broad cross section of diners. Outfitted with Formica-clad tables

Kids **Family-Friendly Restaurants**

Mrs. Wilkes' Boarding House *(see p. 122)* Since your kid didn't grow up in the era of the boardinghouse, here's a chance to experience a long-faded American dining custom. It's an all-you-can-eat type of family-style place. Your kid might balk at the okra and collards, but go for the corn on the cob and barbecued chicken.

Wall's *(see below)* If your kid is from the North and has never tasted Southern barbecue, take him here. There is no finer introduction. Even the booths are plastic. Spareribs and barbecue sandwiches are the hearty fare, but there's also a vegetable plate for the non-meat eater in the family.

and the kind of chairs you'd expect in the lounge of a bowling alley, it occupies cramped no-frills quarters about a block from Oglethorpe Square. You'll be greeted with a broad smile from Nita Dixon or her designated representative (any of a squadron of loyal friends). Then you follow in line to a steam table where simmering portions of Southern food wait delectably. They'll include crab cakes, crab balls, meat loaf, fried chicken, collards, pork or beef ribs, several preparations of okra, butterbeans, yams, and hoecakes (many recipes were handed down from generation to generation through Nita's long line of maternal forebears). Past guests have included Meg Ryan and *People's Court*'s Judge Wapner.

140 Abercorn St. ⓒ **912/238-8233.** Lunch $6.95–$12.95. DISC, MC, V. Mon–Sat 11:30am–2:30pm.

Wall's BARBECUE This is the first choice for anyone seeking the best barbecue in Savannah. Southern barbecue aficionados have built-in radar to find a place like this. Once they see the plastic booths, bibs, Styrofoam cartons, and canned drinks from a fridge, they'll know they've found home. Like all barbecue joints, the place is aggressively casual. Spareribs and barbecue sandwiches star on the menu. Deviled crabs are the only nonbarbecue item, though a vegetable plate of four nonmeat items is also served.

515 E. York Lane (between York St. and Oglethorpe Ave.). ⓒ **912/232-9754.** Reservations not accepted. Main courses $5.50–$7.40. No credit cards. Wed 11am–5pm, Thurs–Sat 11am–9pm.

UND THE CITY MARKET

E

ITALIAN Many of the city's art-conscious students appreciate this Italian cafe because of the fanciful murals adorning its walls. (Painted by the owner's daughter, their theme is defined as "The Jungles of Italy.") If you're looking for a quiet, contemplative evening, we advise you to go elsewhere—the setting is loud and convivial during the early evening and even louder later at night. Designed as a fire station in 1871, it boasts the original pressed-tin ceiling.

Menu items include roasted red peppers with goat-cheese croutons on a bed of wild lettuces, crispy calamari, artichoke hearts with aioli, about a dozen kinds of pasta, and a repertoire of Italian-inspired chicken, veal, and seafood dishes. Daily specials change frequently but sometimes include duck Garibaldi, king-crab fettuccine, and a choice of lusciously fattening desserts.

315 W. Congress St. ℂ **912/232-7118.** Reservations recommended. Main courses $8.95–$24.95. AE, MC, V. Sun–Thurs 5:30–10:30pm, Fri–Sat 5:30pm–midnight.

INEXPENSIVE

606 East Café (Cow Patio) AMERICAN This place reigns as the most irreverent and good-natured restaurant in Savannah, the whimsical creation of owner and muralist Sandi Baumer. A self-described "hater of plain white walls," she combined carloads of 1950s kitsch with tongue-in-cheek testimonials to the proud but passé days of psychedelic rock. Food and drinks are served by Cyndi Lauper lookalikes in short crinoline skirts, and live music is usually featured on a side terrace outfitted like a New Orleans courtyard as viewed through a purple haze. Vegetarian lasagna, burgers, pasta primavera, shrimp tempura, and an "amazing" meat loaf sandwich are some choices.

319 W. Congress St. ℂ **912/233-2887.** Salads, burgers, sandwiches $3–$6.50; platters $6.50–$12.95. AE, MC, V. Mon–Wed 11am–10pm, Thurs–Sat 11am–11pm, Sun noon–10pm.

IN THE VICTORIAN DISTRICT
VERY EXPENSIVE

Elizabeth on 37th ⚥⚥ MODERN SOUTHERN This restaurant is frequently cited as the most glamorous and upscale in town. It's housed in a palatial neoclassical-style 1900 villa ringed with semitropical landscaping and cascades of Spanish moss. The menu items change with the season and manage to retain their gutsy originality despite an elegant presentation. They may include roast quail with mustard-and-pepper sauce and apricot-pecan chutney, herb-seasoned rack of lamb, or broiled salmon with mustard-garlic glaze. You might begin with grilled-eggplant soup, a culinary first for many diners. There's also an impressive wine list, and on Thursday all wines are sold by the glass. The desserts are the best in Savannah.

105 E. 37th St. ⓒ **912/236-5547.** Reservations required. Main courses $23.50–$31.50. AE, DC, DISC, MC, V. Mon–Thurs and Sun 6–9:30pm, Fri–Sat 6–10:30pm.

DINING NEARBY

Johnny Harris Restaurant AMERICAN   Started as a roadside diner in 1924, Johnny Harris is Savannah's oldest continuously operated restaurant. The place has a lingering aura of the 1950s and features all that great food so beloved back in the days of Elvis and Marilyn: barbecue, charbroiled steaks, and seafood. The barbecue pork is especially savory and the prime rib tender. Colonel Sanders never came anywhere close to equaling the fried chicken here. Guests can dine in the "kitchen" or the main dining room and dance under the "stars" in the main dining room on Friday and Saturday nights, when there's live entertainment. The place will make you nostalgic.

1651 Victory Dr. (Hwy. 80). ⓒ **912/354-7810.** Reservations recommended. Jackets required Sat night for dancing. Lunch items $4.95–$7.95; dinner main courses $7.95–$18.95. AE, CB, DC, DISC, MC, V. Mon–Thurs 11:30am–10:30pm, Fri–Sat 11:30am–midnight.

The River's End SEAFOOD   At Tassie's Pier next door to the Thunderbolt Marina on the Intracoastal Waterway, this is a great place to relax and watch shrimp boat and pleasure boat traffic. To the sounds of grand piano music, start with either oysters Rockefeller or Savannah she-crab soup. Charbroiled seafood items include salmon, swordfish, grouper, and tuna, but there's more than fish. You can try chicken Alfredo, charbroiled steaks, succulent lamb, or duck a l'orange. Desserts range from fresh Key lime pie to Georgia bourbon pecan pie.

3122 River Dr. ⓒ **912/354-2973.** Reservations required on Fri and Sat. Full dinners $11.95–$24.95. AE, DC, MC, V. Mon–Thurs 5–10pm, Fri–Sat 5–11pm. Go 5½ miles east on U.S. 80 to Victory Dr., then ½ mile south on River Dr.

5 Seeing the Sights

Most likely, the first sights you'll want to see in Savannah are those mentioned in *Midnight in the Garden of Good and Evil*. So if that's your wish, see "Organized Tours," later in this chapter.

HISTORIC HOMES

Davenport House Museum ☆   This is where seven determined women started the whole Savannah restoration movement in 1954. They raised $22,500, a tidy sum back then, and purchased the house, saving it from demolition and a future as a parking lot. They established the Historic Savannah Foundation, and the whole city was spared. Constructed between 1815 and 1820 by master builder Isaiah Davenport, this is one of the truly great Federal-style houses in the United States, with delicate ironwork and a handsome elliptical stairway.

324 E. State St. ✆ **912/236-8097**. Admission $6 adults, $3 children 6–18; free for children 5 and under. Mon–Sat 10am–4pm, Sun 1–4pm. Closed major holidays.

Green-Meldrim Home ☆   This impressive house was built on Madison Square for cotton merchant Charleston Green, but its moment in history came when it became the Savannah headquarters of Gen. William Tecumseh Sherman at the end of his 1864 "March to the Sea." It was from this Gothic-style house that the general sent his now infamous (at least in Savannah) Christmas telegram to President Lincoln, offering him the city as a Christmas gift. Now the Parish House for St. John's Episcopal Church, the house is open to the public. The former kitchen, servants' quarters, and stable are used as a rectory for the church.

14 W. Macon St. ✆ **912/233-3845**. Admission $5 adults, $3 children. Tues, Thurs and Fri 10am–4pm, Sat 10am–1pm.

Juliette Gordon Low's Birthplace ☆   Juliette Gordon Low— the founder of the Girl Scouts—lived in this Regency-style house that's now maintained both as a memorial to her and as a National Program Center. The Victorian additions to the 1818–21 house were made in 1886, just before Juliette Gordon married William Mackay Low.

142 Bull St. (at Oglethorpe Ave.). ✆ **912/233-4501**. Admission $6 adults, $5 children 18 and under. Mon–Tues and Thurs–Sat 10am–4pm, Sun 12:30–4:30pm. Closed major holidays and some Sun Dec–Jan.

Andrew Low House ☆   After her marriage, Juliette Low (see above) lived in this 1848 house, and it was here where she actually founded the Girl Scouts. She died on the premises in 1927. The classic mid-19th-century house facing Lafayette Square is of stucco over brick with elaborate ironwork, shuttered piazzas, carved woodwork, and crystal chandeliers. William Makepeace Thackeray visited here twice (the desk

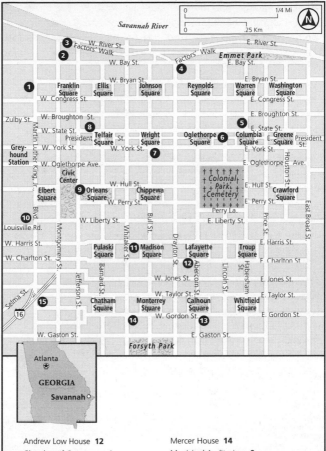

0   1/4 Mi
0   .25 Km

Savannah River

W. River St.   E. River St.
Factors' Walk
W. Bay St.   Factors' Walk   **Emmet Park**   E. Bay St.

W. Bryan St.   E. Bryan St.

Franklin Square   Ellis Square   Johnson Square   Reynolds Square   Warren Square   Washington Square

W. Congress St.   E. Congress St.

W. Broughton St.   E. Broughton St.

Zulby St.   W. State St.   E. State St.

President St.   Telfair Square   Wright Square   Oglethorpe Square   Columbia Square   Greene Square   President St.

Grey-hound Station   W. York St.   W. York St.   E. York St.

W. Oglethorpe Ave.   E. Oglethorpe Ave.   Houston St.

Civic Center

W. Hull St.   E. Hull St.

Elbert Square   Orleans Square   Chippewa Square   Colonial Park Cemetery   Crawford Square

W. Perry St.   Perry La.   E. Perry St.

W. Liberty St.   E. Liberty St.

Louisville Rd.   Montgomery St.   Whitaker St.   Bull St.   Drayton St.   Price St.   East Broad St.

W. Harris St.   E. Harris St.

W. Charlton St.   Pulaski Square   Madison Square   Lafayette Square   Troup Square   E. Charlton St.

Barnard St.   Abercorn St.   Lincoln St.   Habersham St.

W. Jones St.   E. Jones St.

Jefferson St.   W. Taylor St.   E. Taylor St.

Selma St.   Chatham Square   Monterrey Square   Calhoun Square   Whitfield Square

16   W. Gordon St.   E. Gordon St.

W. Gaston St.   E. Gaston St.

Forsyth Park

Atlanta

GEORGIA

Savannah

Andrew Low House **12**

Chamber of Commerce **4**

Davenport House Museum **5**

Factors' Walk **3**

First African Baptist Church **2**

Green-Meldrim Home **11**

Juliette Gordon Low's Birthplace **7**

Massie Heritage Interpretation Center **13**

Mercer House **14**

Municipal Auditorium **9**

Owen-Thomas House & Museum **6**

Ralph Mark Gilbert Civil Rights Museum **15**

Savannah History Museum **10**

Ships of the Sea Maritime Museum **1**

Telfair Mansion & Art Museum **8**

Savannah Visitor Center **10**

at which he worked is in one bedroom), and Robert E. Lee was entertained at a gala reception in the double parlors in 1870.

329 Abercorn St. ℂ **912/233-6854.** Admission $7 adults; $4.50 students, children 6–12, and Girl Scouts; free for children 5 and under. Mon–Wed and Fri–Sat 10:30am–4pm, Sun noon–3:30pm. Closed major holidays.

Telfair Mansion and Art Museum ⚜   The oldest public art museum in the South, housing a collection of both American and European paintings, was designed and built by William Jay in 1818. He was a young English architect noted for introducing the Regency style to America. The house was built for Alexander Telfair, son of Edward Telfair, the governor of Georgia. A sculpture gallery and rotunda were added in 1883, and Jefferson Davis, former president of the Confederacy, attended the formal opening in 1886. William Jay's period rooms have been restored, and the Octagon Room and Dining Room are particularly outstanding.

121 Bernard St. ℂ **912/232-1177.** Admission $6 adults, $2 students, $1 children 6–12, free for children 5 and under. Mon noon–5pm, Tues–Sat 10am–5pm, Sun 1–5pm.

Owen-Thomas House and Museum ⚜⚜   Famed as a place where Lafayette spent the night in 1825, this house evokes the heyday of Savannah's golden age. It was designed in 1816 by English architect William Jay, who captured the grace of Georgian Bath in England and the splendor of Regency London. The place has been called a "jewel box." You can visit not only the bedchambers and kitchen but also the garden and the drawing and dining rooms. Adapted from the original slave quarters and stable, the Carriage House Visitors' Center opened in 1995.

124 Abercorn St. ℂ **912/233-9743.** Admission $8 adults, $4 students, $2 children 6–12, free for children 5 and under. Mon noon–5pm, Tues–Sat 10am–5pm, Sun 2–5pm.

MUSEUMS

Savannah History Museum ⚜   Housed in the restored train shed of the old Central Georgia Railway station, this museum is a good introduction to the city. In the theater, *The Siege of Savannah* is replayed. An exhibition hall displays memorabilia from every era of Savannah's history.

303 Martin Luther King Jr. Blvd. ℂ **912/238-1779.** Admission $3 adults, $2.50 seniors, $1.75 students. Daily 8:30am–5pm.

Ships of the Sea Maritime Museum ⚜   This museum has intricately constructed models of seagoing vessels from Viking

Martinis in the Cemetery

All fans of *Midnight in the Garden of Good and Evil* must pay a visit to the now world-famous **Bonaventure Cemetery,** filled with obelisks and columns and dense shrubbery and moss-draped trees. Bonaventure is open daily 8am to 5pm. You get there by taking Wheaton Street east out of downtown to Bonaventure Road. (You don't want to approach it by boat like Minerva the "voodoo priestess" and John Berendt did—and certainly not anywhere near midnight.)

This cemetery lies on the grounds of what was once a great oak-shaded plantation, built by Col. John Mulryne. In the late 1700s, the mansion caught fire during a formal dinner party; reportedly, the host quite calmly led his guests from the dining room and into the garden, where they settled in to finish eating while the house burned to the ground in front of them. At the end, the host and the guests threw their crystal glasses against the trunk of an old oak tree. It's said that on still nights you can still hear the laughter and the crashing of the crystal. In The Book, Mary Harty called the ruins the "scene of the Eternal Party. What better place, in Savannah, to rest in peace for all time—where the party goes on and on."

It was at the cemetery that John Berendt had martinis in silver goblets with Miss Harty, while they sat on the bench-gravestone of poet **Conrad Aiken.** She pointed out to the writer the double gravestone bearing the names of Dr. William F. Aiken and his wife, Anna, parents of Conrad. They both died on February 27, 1901, when Dr. Aiken killed his wife and then himself. The Aikens are buried in plot H-48. Songwriter **Johnny Mercer** is also buried in plot H-48. But not **Danny Hansford,** the blond hustler of the book. You can find his grave at plot G-19 in the Greenwich Cemetery, next to Bonaventure. After entering Bonaventure, turn left immediately and take the straight path to Greenwich. Eventually you'll see a small granite tile:

DANNY LEW HANSFORD
MARCH 1, 1960
MAY 2, 1981

Incidentally, **Jim Williams** is buried in Gordon, Georgia, a 3½-hour drive northwest of Savannah.

warships right up to today's nuclear-powered ships. In models ranging from the size of your fist to 8 feet in length, you can see such famous ships as the *Mayflower* and the *Savannah,* the first steamship to cross the Atlantic. More than 75 ships are in the museum's ship-in-a-bottle collection, most of them constructed by Peter Barlow, a retired British Royal Naval commander.

41 Martin Luther King Jr. Blvd. ⓒ **912/232-1511.** Admission $5 adults, $4 children 7–12, free for children 6 and under. Tues–Sun 10am–5pm. Closed major holidays.

LITERARY LANDMARKS

Long before John Berendt's *Midnight in the Garden of Good and Evil,* there were other writers who were associated with Savannah.

Chief of these was **Flannery O'Connor** (1924–64), one of the South's greatest writers, author of *Wise Blood* (1952) and *The Violent Bear It Away* (1960). She was also known for her short stories, including the collection *A Good Man Is Hard to Find* (1955). She won the O. Henry Award three times. Between October and May, an association dedicated to her holds readings, films, and lectures about her and other Southern writers. You can visit the **Flannery O'Connor Childhood Home,** 207 E. Charlton St. (ⓒ **912/233-6014**). The house is open only Saturday and Sunday from 1 to 4pm. Admission is free.

Conrad Aiken (1889–1973), the American poet, critic, writer, and Pulitzer Prize winner, was also born in Savannah. He lived at 228 (for the first 11 years of his life) and also at 230 E. Oglethorpe Ave. (for the last 11 years of his life). In *Midnight in the Garden of Good and Evil,* Mary Harty and its author sipped martinis at the bench-shaped tombstone of Aiken in Bonaventure Cemetery (see "Martinis in the Cemetery," above).

Mercer House, 429 Bull St., featured in The Book, is not open to the public. Many of its most elegant contents were auctioned off at Sotheby's in October 2000 for $1 million, including the Anatolian carpet upon which the hapless Danny Hansford is reputed to have fallen after being shot. The house was recently up for sale ($9 million), but failed to snag a buyer and has since been taken off the market. Still, it's been called "the envy of Savannah," and thousands of visitors stop by to photograph it. For more details on the house and the events that took place in it, see the "Ghost Talk Ghost Walk" walking tour at the end of this section.

BLACK HISTORY SIGHTS

Savannah boasts the **First African Baptist Church,** 23 Montgomery St., Franklin Sq. (ⓒ **912/233-6597**), the first such church in North America. It was established by George Leile, a slave whose master allowed him to preach to other slaves when they made visits to plantations along the Savannah River. Leile was granted his freedom in 1777 and later raised some $1,500 to purchase the present church from a white congregation. The black congregation rebuilt the church brick by brick, and it became the first brick building in Georgia to be owned by African Americans. The pews on either side of the organ are the work of African slaves. Morning worship is at 11:30am daily.

Ralph Mark Gilbert Civil Rights Museum, 460 Martin Luther King Jr. Blvd. (© **912/231-8900**), close to the Savannah Visitors Center, opened in 1996. It's dedicated to the life and service of African Americans and their contributions to the civil-rights movements in Savannah. Dr. Gilbert died in 1956 but was a leader in early efforts to gain educational, social, and political equity for African Americans in Savannah. Hours are Monday to Saturday 9am to 5pm. Admission is $4 for adults, $3 for seniors, and $2 for children.

NEARBY FORTS

About 2½ miles east of the center of Savannah via the Islands Expressway stands **Old Fort Jackson,** 1 Fort Jackson Rd. (© **912/232-3945**), Georgia's oldest standing fort, with a 9-foot-deep tidal moat around its brick walls. In 1775, an earthen battery was built here. The original brick fort was begun in 1808 and manned during the War of 1812. It was enlarged and strengthened between 1845 and 1860 and saw its greatest use as headquarters for the Confederate river defenses during the Civil War. Its arched rooms, designed to support the weight of heavy cannons mounted above, hold 13 exhibit areas. The fort is open daily 9am to 5pm, charging $3.50 for adults and $2.50 for seniors and children 6 to 18; children 5 and under are free.

Fort McAllister, Richmond Hill, 10 miles southwest on U.S. 17 (© **912/727-2339**), on the banks of the Great Ogeechee River, was a Confederate earthwork fortification. Constructed in 1861–62, it withstood nearly 2 years of bombardments before it finally fell on December 13, 1864, in a bayonet charge that ended General Sherman's infamous "March to the Sea." There's a visitor center with historic exhibits and also walking trails and campsites. It's open Tuesday to Saturday 9am to 5pm and Sunday 2 to 5pm. Admission is $2.50 for adults, $1.50 for children over 5, and $2 for seniors.

Fort Pulaski (© 912/786-5787), a national monument, is 15 miles east of Savannah off U.S. 80 on Cockspur and McQueen islands at the very mouth of the Savannah River. It cost $1 million and took 25 tons of brick and 18 years of toil to finish. Yet it was captured in just 30 hours by Union forces. Completed in 1847 with walls 7½ feet thick, it was taken by Georgia forces at the beginning of the war. However, on April 11, 1862, defense strategy changed worldwide when Union cannons, firing from more than a mile away on Tybee Island, overcame the masonry fortification. The effectiveness of rifled artillery (firing a bullet-shaped projectile with great accuracy at long range) was clearly demonstrated. The new Union weapon marked the end of the era of masonry fortifications. The fort was pentagon shaped, with galleries and drawbridges crossing the moat. You can still find shells from 1862 imbedded in the walls. There are exhibits of the fort's history in the visitor center. It's open daily (except Christmas) 8:30am to 6:45pm. Admission is $2 for adults and free to those 16 and under, with a $4 maximum per car.

ESPECIALLY FOR KIDS

Massie Heritage Interpretation Center   Here's a stop in the Historic District for the kids. Geared to school-age children, the center features various exhibits about Savannah, including such subjects as the city's Greek, Roman, and Gothic architecture; the Victorian era; and a history of public education. Other exhibits include a period costume room and a 19th-century classroom, where children can experience a classroom environment from days gone by.

207 E. Gordon St. © 912/201-5070. Admission free, but $2 donation requested. Mon–Fri 9am–4pm.

6 Organized Tours

If it's a *Midnight in the Garden of Good and Evil* tour you seek, then you've obviously come to the right place. Virtually every tour group in town offers tours of the *Midnight* sites, many of which are included on their regular agenda. Ask any of the tour groups here about their tours. Note that some tour outfits will accommodate only groups, so if you're traveling alone or as a pair, be sure to make that known when you make your tour reservations.

A delightful way to see Savannah is by horse-drawn carriage. An authentic antique carriage carries you over cobblestone streets as the coachman spins a tale of the town's history. The 1-hour tour ($17 for adults, $8 for children) covers 15 of the 20 squares. Reservations are required, so contact **Carriage Tours of Savannah** at ℭ **912/ 236-6756.**

Old Town Trolley Tours (ℭ **912/233-0083**) operates tours of the Historic District, with pickups at most downtown inns and hotels ($21 for adults, $8 for children 4 to 12), as well as a 1-hour **Haunted History** tour detailing Savannah's ghostly past (and present). Call to reserve for all tours.

Gray Line Savannah Tours (ℭ **912/236-9604**) has joined forces with **Historic Savannah Foundation Tours** (ℭ **912/234-TOUR**) to feature narrated bus tours of museums, squares, parks, and homes. Reservations must be made for all tours, and most have starting points at the visitor center and pickup points at various hotels and motels. Tours cost $19 for adults and $8 for children 11 and under.

Negro Heritage Trail Tour, 502 E. Harris St. (ℭ **912/ 234-8000**), offers organized tours ($15 for adults and $7 for children) from the African-American perspective. The trail is sponsored by the King-Tinsdell Cottage Foundation.

Savannah Riverboat Cruises are offered aboard the *Savannah River Queen,* operated by the River Street Riverboat Co., 9 E. River St. (ℭ **800/786-6404** or 912/232-6404). You get a glimpse of Savannah as Oglethorpe saw it back in 1733. You'll see the historic cotton warehouses lining River Street and the statue of the *Waving Girl* as the huge modern freighters see it as they arrive daily at Savannah. Lunch and bar service are available. Adults pay $15, and children 12 and under are charged $9.16.

Ghost Talk Ghost Walk takes you through colonial Savannah on a journey filled with stories and legends based on Margaret Debolt's book *Savannah Spectres and Other Strange Tales.* If you're not a believer at the beginning of the guided tour, you may be at the end. The tour starts at Reynolds Square. For information, contact Jack Richards at New Forest Studios, 127 E. Congress St. (ℭ **912/ 233-3896**). Hours for tour departures can vary. The cost is $10 for adults and $5 for children.

Low Country River Excursions, a narrated nature cruise, leaves from the Bull River Marina, 8005 Old Tybee Rd. (U.S. 80 East). Call ℭ **912/898-9222** for information. Passengers are taken on a 1993 38-foot pontoon boat, *Natures Way,* for an encounter with the friendly bottle-nosed dolphin. Both scenery and wildlife unfold during the 90-minute cruise down the Bull River. Trips are possible daily at 2 and 4pm and sunset spring through fall, weather permitting. Adults pay $15, seniors $12, and children 11 and under $10. There's a 30-passenger limit.

7 Outdoor Pursuits

BIKING   Savannah doesn't usually have a lot of heavy traffic except during rush hours, so you can bicycle up and down the streets of the Historic District, visiting as many of the green squares as you wish. There's no greater city bicycle ride in all the state of Georgia.

In lieu of a local bike-rental shop, many inns and hotels will provide bikes for their guests.

CAMPING   The **Bellaire Woods Campground,** 805 Fort Argyle Rd. (© **912/748-4000**), is 2½ miles west of I-95, 4½ miles west of U.S. 17, and 12 miles from the Savannah Historic District on the banks of the Ogeechee River. Facilities include full hookups, LP gas service, a store, self-service gas and diesel fuel, a dump station, hot showers, a laundry, and a pool. Rates range from $22.50 for tents to $27.50 for RV hookups, and reservations are accepted with a $10 deposit.

Open year-round, **Skidaway Island State Park** (© **912/598-2300**) offers 88 camping sites with full hookups, costing $17. On arrival, you purchase a $2 parking pass valid for your entire stay. The grounds include 1- and 3-mile nature trails, grills, picnic tables, a pool, a bathhouse, and a laundry. Also open year-round, the **River's End Campground and RV Park,** Polk Street, Tybee Island (© **912/786-5518**), consists of 128 sites featuring full hookups, with groceries and a beach nearby. Tent sites cost $18 per day and RV sites $24 per day.

DIVING   The **Diving Locker-Ski Chalet,** 74 W. Montgomery Cross Rd. (© **912/927-6604**), offers a wide selection of equipment and services for various water sports. Scuba classes cost $230 for a series of weekday evening lessons and $245 for a series of lessons beginning on Friday evening. A full scuba-gear package, including buoyancy-control device, tank, and wet suit, goes for $49. You must provide your own snorkel, mask, fins, and booties. It's open Monday to Friday 10am to 6pm and Saturday 10am to 5pm.

FISHING   **Amicks Deep Sea Fishing,** 6902 Sand Nettles Dr. (© **912/897-6759**), offers daily charters featuring a 41-foot 1993 custom-built boat. The rate is $85 per person and includes rod, reel, bait, and tackle. Bring your own lunch, though beer and soda are sold on board. Reservations are recommended, but if you show up 30 minutes before scheduled departure, there may be space available. Daily departures from the Bull River Marina, 8005 Old Tybee Rd. (U.S. 80 East), are at 7am, with returns at 6pm.

Exploring the Savannah National Wildlife Refuge

A 10-minute drive across the river from downtown Savannah delivers you to the wild, even though you can see the city's industrial and port complexes in the background. The **Savannah National Wildlife Refuge** 🎋🎋🎋 (📞 **912/652-4415**), which overflows into South Carolina, was the site of rice plantations in the 1800s and is today a wide expanse of woodland and marsh, ideal for a scenic drive, a canoe ride, a picnic, and most definitely a look at a variety of animals.

From Savannah, get on U.S. Highway 17A, crossing the Talmadge Bridge. It's about 8 miles to the intersection of hwys. 17 and 17A, where you turn left toward the airport. You'll see the refuge entrance, marked Laurel Hill Wildlife Drive, after going some 2 miles. Inside the gate to the refuge is a visitor center, distributing maps and leaflets.

Laurel Hill Wildlife Drive goes on for 4 miles or so. It's possible to bike along this trail. People come here mainly to spy on the alligators, and sightings are almost guaranteed. However, other creatures in the wild abound, including bald eagles and otters. Hikers can veer off the drive and go along Cistern Trail, leading to Recess Island. Because the trail is marked, there's little danger of getting lost.

Nearly 40 miles of dikes are open to birders and backpackers. Canoeists float along tidal creeks, which are fingers of the Savannah River. Fishing and hunting are allowed in special conditions and in the right season. Deer and squirrel are commonplace; rarer is the feral hog known along coastal Georgia and South Carolina.

Visits are possible daily sunrise to sunset. For more information, write the Savannah National Wildlife Refuge, U.S. Fish & Wildlife Service, Savannah Coastal Refuges, P.O. Box 8487, Savannah, GA 31412.

GOLF   Bacon Park, Shorty Cooper Drive (📞 **912/354-2625**), is a 27-hole course with greens fees of $18 for an 18-hole round. Carts can be rented for an additional $9.50. Golf facilities include a lighted driving range, putting greens, and a pro shop. It's open daily dawn to dusk.

Henderson Golf Club, 1 Henderson Dr. (© **912/920-4653**), includes an 18-hole championship course, a lighted driving range, a PGA professional staff, and golf instruction and schools. The greens fees are $40 Monday to Friday and $42 Saturday and Sunday. It's open daily 7:30am to 10pm.

Another option is the 9-hole **Mary Calder,** West Congress Street (© **912/238-7100**), where the greens fees are $13 per day Monday to Friday and $11 per day Saturday and Sunday. It's open daily 7:30am to 7pm (to 5:30pm in winter).

IN-LINE SKATING At **Diving Locker-Ski Chalet** (see "Diving," above), skate rentals cost $12 for 4 hours and $20 for a full day, with a Friday-to-Monday rental going for $35.

JET SKIING At **Bull River Marina,** 8005 Old Tybee Rd., Hwy. 80 East(© **912/897-7300**), you can rent one-, two-, or three-seater jet skis. Prices, regardless of how many seats, rent for $30 per half hour or $60 per hour. It's open daily 9am to 6pm. Reservations are recommended.

JOGGING "The most beautiful city to jog in"—that's how the president of the Savannah Striders Club characterizes Savannah. He's correct. The historic avenues provide an exceptional setting for your run. The Convention & Visitors Bureau can provide you with a map outlining three of the Striders Club's routes: Heart of Savannah YMCA Course, 3.1 miles; Symphony Race Course, 5 miles; and the Children's Run Course, 5 miles.

NATURE WATCHES Explore the wetlands with **Palmetto Coast Charters,** Lazaretto Creek Marina, Tybee Island (© **912/ 786-5403**). Charters include trips to the Barrier Islands for shell collecting and watches for otter, mink, birds, and other wildlife. The captain is a naturalist and a professor, so he can answer your questions. Palmetto also features a dolphin watch usually conducted daily 4:30 to 6:30pm, when the shrimp boats come in with dolphins following behind. The cost is $100 for up to six people for a minimum of 2 hours, plus $50 for each extra hour.

RECREATIONAL PARKS **Bacon Park** (see "Golf," above, and "Tennis," below) includes 1,021 acres with archery, golf, tennis, and baseball fields. **Daffin Park,** 1500 E. Victory Dr. (© **912/ 351-3851**), features playgrounds, soccer, tennis, basketball, baseball, a pool, a lake pavilion, and picnic grounds. Both of these parks are open daily: May to September 8am to 11pm and October to April 8am to 10pm.

Located at Montgomery Cross Road and Sallie Mood Drive, **Lake Mayer Park** (℃ **912/652-6780**) consists of 75 acres featuring a multitude of activities, such as public fishing and boating, lighted jogging and bicycle trails, a playground, and pedal-boat rentals.

SAILING   Sail Harbor, 618 Wilmington Island Rd. (℃ **912/ 897-2896**), features the Catalina 25 boat, costing $100 per half day and $140 per full day, with an extra day costing $80. A Saturday and Sunday outing goes for $200. It's open Tuesday to Saturday 10am to 6pm and Sunday 12:30 to 5:30pm.

TENNIS   Bacon Park (see "Golf," above, ℃ **912/351-3850**) offers 14 lighted courts open Monday to Thursday 9am to 9pm, Friday 9am to 4pm and 5 to 8pm, and Saturday 9am to 1am. **Forsyth Park,** at Drayton and Gaston streets (℃ **912/351-3850**), has four courts open daily 7am to 9pm. Both parks charge $1.75 per hour during the day and $2.50 per hour after 5pm. The use of the eight lighted courts at **Lake Mayer Park,** Montgomery Cross Road, costs nothing. These courts are open daily 8am to 11pm.

8 Shopping

River Street is a shopper's delight, with some nine blocks (including Riverfront Plaza) of interesting shops, offering everything from crafts to clothing to souvenirs. The **City Market,** between Ellis and Franklin squares on West St. Julian Street, boasts art galleries, boutiques, and sidewalk cafes along with a horse-and-carriage ride. Bookstores, boutiques, and antiques shops are located between Wright Square and Forsyth Park.

Oglethorpe Mall, at 7804 Abercorn St., has more than 100 specialty shops and four major department stores, as well as restaurants and fast-food outlets. The **Savannah Mall,** 14045 Abercorn St., is Savannah's newest shopping center, offering two floors of shopping. Included on the premises is a food court with its own carousel. The anchor stores are J.B. White, Montgomery Ward, Parisian, and Belk.

Some 30 manufacturer-owned "factory direct" stores offer savings up to 70% at the **Savannah Festival Factory Stores,** Abercorn Street at I-95 (℃ **912/925-3089**). Shops feature national brand names of shoes, luggage, gifts, cosmetics, household items, toys, and clothing, including T-shirts Plus and the Duckhead Outlet.

ANTIQUES

Alex Raskin Antiques   This shop offers a wide array of antiques of varying ages. The selection includes everything from accessories to furniture, rugs, and paintings. 441 Bull St. (in the Noble Hardee Mansion), Monterey Square. ℂ **912/232-8205.**

J. D. Weed & Co.   This shop prides itself on providing "that wonderful treasure that combines history and personal satisfaction with rarity and value." If you're looking for a particular item, just let the staff know and they'll try to find it for you. 102 W. Victory Dr. ℂ **912/234-8540.**

Memory Lane   More than 8,000 square feet of collectibles can be found here. The specialty of the house is a collection of German sleds and wagons. You'll also find glassware, furniture, and pottery. 230 W. Bay St. ℂ **912/232-0975.**

ART & SCULPTURE

Gallery 209   Housed in an 1820s cotton warehouse, this gallery displays two floors of original paintings by local artists, sculpture, woodworking, fiber art, gold and silver jewelry, enamels, photography, batiks, pottery, and stained glass. You'll also find a wide selection of limited-edition reproductions and note cards of local scenes. 209 E. River St. ℂ **912/236-4583.**

The Greek Festival   Many of the clients of this unusual store consider it a valuable resource for the creation of stage or movie sets, fashion displays, or dramatic living spaces. Co-owner Kelli Johnson acquires the molds for pieces of ancient Greek and Roman sculpture, Baroque or Victorian wall brackets, or carved animals (everything from Chinese Foo dogs to giant tortoises bearing tufted cushions for use as coffee tables). Everything is cast in reinforced plaster or concrete, which makes the price a fraction of what it would have been if the objects had been carved individually. The store can arrange shipping to virtually anywhere, and if what you want isn't in stock, you can order from a voluminous catalog. 143 Bull St. ℂ **912/234-8984.**

John Tucker Fine Arts   This gallery offers museum-quality pieces by local artists as well as those from around the world, including Haitian and Mexican craftspeople. In a restored 1800s home, the gallery features 19th- and 20th-century landscapes, marine-art painting, portraits, folk art, and still life. 5 W. Charlton St. ℂ **800/ 350-1401** or 912/231-8161. www.tuckerfinearts.com.

Morning Star Gallery   This gallery features the works of more than 80 artists. Pieces include hand-thrown pottery, metalwork, paintings, prints, woodworks, jewelry, and glass (hand-blown and leaded). 8 E. Liberty St. ✆ **912/233-4307.**

Village Craftsmen   This collection of artisans offers a wide array of handmade crafts, including hand-blown glass, needlework, folk art, limited-edition prints, restored photographs, and hand-thrown pottery. 223 W. River St. ✆ **912/236-7280.**

BLACKSMITH

Walsh Mountain Ironworks   This is the sales outlet of the most successful and high-profile blacksmith in Savannah. Inventories include house, kitchen, and garden ornaments, many of which have modern, but vaguely Gothic, designs. Objects for sale include headboards for beds, garden arbors, trellises, tables, chairs, wine racks, CD racks, and ornamental screens. Prices range from $4 to $1,600, and in some cases require several weeks waiting time. 427 Whitaker St. ✆ **912/239-9818.**

BOOKS

Book Warehouse   This store offers more than 75,000 titles, including fiction, cookbooks, children's books, computer manuals, and religious tomes. Prices begin at less than a dollar, and all proceeds are donated to Emory University for cancer research. 8705 Abercorn St. ✆ **912/927-0824.**

E. Shaver, Bookseller   Housed on the ground floor of a Greek Revival mansion, E. Shaver features 12 rooms of tomes. Specialties include architecture, decorative arts, regional history, and children's books as well as 17th-, 18th-, and 19th-century maps. 326 Bull St. ✆ **912/234-7257.**

CANDY & OTHER FOODS

Plantation Sweets Vidalia Onions   Outside Savannah, check out the Vidalia onion specialties offered by the Collins family for more than 50 years. Sample one of the relishes, dressings, or gift items as well. Call for directions. Rte. 2, Cobbtown. ✆ **800/541-2272.**

River Street Sweets   Begun more than 20 years ago as part of the River Street restoration project, this store offers a wide selection of candies, including pralines, bearclaws, fudge, and chocolates. Included among the specialties are more than 30 flavors of taffy made on a machine from the early 1900s. 13 E. River St. ✆ **800/ 627-6175** or 912/234-4608.

Savannah's Candy Kitchen Chocolate-dipped Oreos, glazed pecans, pralines, and fudge are only a few of the delectables at this confectionery. While enjoying one of the candies or ice creams, you can watch the taffy machine in action. Staff members are so sure you'll be delighted with their offerings that they offer a full money-back guarantee if not satisfied. 225 E. River St. ℂ **800/242-7919** or 912/233-8411.

GIFTS & COLLECTIBLES

Candlesticks Kalten Bach owns this candle-making place. You can watch a candle being made from beginning to end in about 15 minutes at demonstrations held throughout the day. All personnel train for roughly a year before they can create their own pieces. 117 E. River St. ℂ **912/231-9041**.

Charlotte's Corner Featuring local items, this shop offers a wide array of gifts and souvenirs. The selection encompasses children's clothing, a few food items, Sheila houses, and Savannah-related books, including guidebooks and Southern cookbooks. 1 W. Liberty St. (at Bull St.). ℂ **912/233-8061**.

Bothwell Gallery In the Historic District, this shop features more than 40 artists from throughout the Southeast. You'll find wall hangings, pottery, jewelry, clothing, furniture, and sculptures. 422 Whitaker St. ℂ **912/233-5132**.

The Christmas Shop This shop keeps the Christmas spirit alive all year with a large selection of ornaments, Santas, nutcrackers, and collectibles. Collectors will appreciate the various featured lines, including Dept 56, Polonaise, Christina's World, and Patricia Breen. 307 Bull St. ℂ **912/234-5343**.

Enchantments If you collect bears and dolls, this store has a pet for you. Among its other selections is an array of quality toys and collector's pieces. 311 Bull St. (at Madison Sq.). ℂ **912/651-9035**.

JEWELRY & SILVER

Levy Jewelers Located downtown, this boutique deals mainly in antique jewelry. It offers a large selection of gold, silver, gems, and watches. Among its other items are crystal, china, and gift items. 4711 Waters Ave. ℂ **912/238-2125**.

Simply Silver The specialty here is sterling flatware, ranging from today's designs to discontinued items of yesteryear. The inventory includes new and estate pieces along with a wide array of gift items. 14-A Bishop Court. ℂ **912/238-3652**.

9 Savannah After Dark

River Street, along the Savannah River, is the major after-dark venue. Many night owls stroll the waterfront until they hear the sound of music they like, then follow their ears inside.

In summer, concerts of jazz, Big Band, and Dixieland music fill downtown **Johnson Square** with lots of foot-tapping sounds that thrill both locals and visitors. Some of Savannah's finest musicians perform regularly on this historic site.

THE PERFORMING ARTS

The **Savannah Symphony Orchestra** has city-sponsored concerts in addition to its regular ticketed events. To spread a blanket in Forsyth Park and listen to the symphony perform beneath the stars or be on River Street on the Fourth of July when the group sends rousing strains echoing across the river is to be transported.

The orchestra is one of two fully professional orchestras in the state of Georgia, and its regular nine-concert masterworks series is presented in the Savannah Civic Center's **Johnny Mercer Theater,** Orleans Square (© **800/537-7894** or 912/236-9536), which is also home to ballet, musicals, and Broadway shows. Call to find out what's being presented at the time of your visit. Tickets range from $20 to $50.

Savannah Theater, Chippewa Square (© **912/233-7764**), presents contemporary plays. Tickets are usually $15 for regular admission and $12 for seniors or students.

September brings the 5-day **Savannah Jazz Festival** (© **912/232-2222**), with nationally known musicians appearing around the city.

LIVE-MUSIC CLUBS

Dejà Groove The setting is a severe-looking 19th-century warehouse that's perched on soaring bulwarks on the sloping embankment between River Walk and the busy traffic of Bay Street. Inside, you'll find an intriguing blend of exposed brick and timber, psychedelic artwork, and a youthful (under 35-ish) sense of hip. There's a dance floor featuring dance music from the '70s and '80s, at least two sprawling bar areas, video games, and about a dozen pool tables, priced at $1 per game. Entrance is usually free, but sometimes a $3 cover charge is levied after 10pm. Open Tuesday to Thursday 8:30pm to 3am, Friday and Saturday 8pm to 3am. 301 Williamson St. © 912/644-4566.

Hannah's East This club, the most popular in Savannah, is the showcase for jazz greats, including Gina Rene and Emma Kelly, "The Lady of 6,000 Songs" who appeared in *Midnight in the Garden of Good and Evil.* Jim Belt is on the scene as the club's new musical director, replacing Ben Tucker (who left for the Lion's Den at the DeSoto Hilton). Emma holds forth Tuesday to Sunday 6 to 9pm. A Monday special features authentic Dixieland and New Orleans–style jazz, beginning at 6pm. At the Pirates' House, 20 E. Broad St. ℂ 912/233-2225. Cover $3–$5 Fri–Sat after 9pm.

Planters Tavern This is Savannah's most beloved tavern, graced with a sprawling and convivial bar, a pair of fireplaces, and a decor of antique bricks and carefully polished hardwoods. Because it's in the cellar of the Olde Pink House, many guests ask that platters of food be served at any of the tavern's tables. Otherwise, you can sit, drink in hand, listening to the melodies emanating from the sadder-but-wiser pianist. Foremost among the divas who perform is the endearingly elegant Gail Thurmond, one of Savannah's most legendary songstresses, who weaves her enchantment Tuesday to Sunday night. In the Olde Pink House Restaurant, 23 Abercorn St. ℂ 912/232-4286. No cover.

Velvet Elvis For two years in a row, this has been Savannah's number-one live music venue, as noted in Savannah's *Creative Loafing* magazine. It's known as punk rock heaven to its hundreds of local fans, with a battered but prominent stage for live bands, and a wrap-around collection of rock 'n' roll memorabilia and kitsch. Until its current manifestation, it was a hippie-style junk store; now you're likely to find such luminaries as Kevin Spacey, John Cusack, and Tracey Cunningham. There's a cover charge, applicable only when music is playing, of between $3 and $10, depending on the band. Open Monday to Saturday from 5pm to 3am. 127 W. Congress St. ℂ 912/236-0665.

The Zoo In its way, it's wilder, less inhibited, and a bit more insid-erish even than Club One, with which it's frequently compared. One thing it isn't—prissy—as you'll quickly realize after a view of its two-fisted clientele (both male and female) and the staggeringly comprehensive array of almost psychedelic cocktails. (One of the house specials, bluntly identified as a Red-Headed Slut, elevated Jagermeister into something mind-bending for between $3 and $4, depending on the size.) If there's a genuine fetishist in Savannah, chances are high that you'll find him, her, or it at this ode to

Southern heat. Expect a scattering of military men on furlough, women and men of slightly untidy morality, a dance venue that's devoted to trance and techno music upstairs, and more conservative top-40 hits on the street level. Open Wednesday to Saturday 9pm until 3am. 121 W. Congress St. ② **912/236-6266**. Cover $5–$10 after 10pm.

BARS & PUBS

Churchill's Pub   If you like a cigar with your martini (the pub has a large selection), this is the place for you. It's the oldest bar in Savannah, having originally been built in England in 1860, dismantled, and shipped to Savannah in the 1920s. On tap are such imported beers as John Courage, Guinness, Dry Blackthorn, and Bass Ale. You can also order pub grub like fish-and-chips, home-made bangers (English sausage), or shepherd's pie. The pub is open daily Monday to Saturday 11:30am to 2am and Sunday 5pm to 2am. Fans of The Movie will recall this pub; fans of The Book will recall the erroneous placement of this pub in The Movie. 9 Drayton St. (1 block south of Bay St.). ② **912/232-8501**.

Crystal Beer Parlor   This historic haunt opened its doors in 1933 and sold huge sandwiches for a dime. Prices have gone up since then, but local affection for this unpretentious place has diminished not one whit. Try to go earlier or later than the peak lunch or dinner hours (if you get there at noon, you'll be in for a lengthy wait). Owner Conrad Thomson still serves up fried oysters and shrimp-salad sandwiches, crab stew, and chili. The seafood gumbo is one of the best in the southern Atlantic region. It's open Monday to Saturday 11am to 9pm. Parking is available in the lot off Jones Street. 301 W. Jones St. (west of Bull St.). ② **912/232-1153**.

Kevin Barry's Irish Pub   The place to be on St. Patrick's Day, this waterfront pub rocks all year. Traditional Irish folk music will entertain you as you choose from a menu featuring such Irish fare as beef stew, shepherd's pie, and corned beef and cabbage. Many folks come here just to drink, often making a night of it in the convivial atmosphere. It's open Monday to Friday 4pm to 3am and Saturday and Sunday 11am to 3pm. 117 W. River St. ② **912/233-9626**. www.kevinbarrys.com. $2 cover.

Mellow Mushroom   Don't expect grandeur here: a member of a Georgia-based restaurant chain, it appeals to a funky, irreverent, and sometimes raucous crowd of college students and faded counter-culture aficionados from yesterday. Decor includes rambling murals painted with an individualized—and subjective—iconography that might require an explanation from a member of the cheerful waitstaff. There's the cut-off front end of a VW beetle near the entrance, a limited menu that focuses almost exclusively on pizzas, salads, and calzones, and a die-hard emphasis on cheap beer, especially Pabst, which sells by the pitcher. Expects lots of SCAD students, a battered, dimly lit interior, recorded (not live) music, and a vague allegiance to the hard rock, hard drugs, and hard sex fantasies of the early 1970s. 11 Liberty St. ℭ **912/495-0705.**

Mercury Lounge   The venue is as hip, counterculture, and art-fully kitsch as anything you might have expected in Manhattan, with the added benefit of a reputation for the biggest martinis (10 ounces) in town. You'll find the most comfortable barstools any-where (they're covered in *faux* leopard or zebra); a house band (the Mercury Lounge Combo) that cranks out their own version of the latest favorites; and, when the band is not performing, a jukebox. Everything is congenially battered, with enough rock and musical memorabilia to please the curators of a rock 'n' roll hall of fame. It's open from 3pm to 3am Monday to Saturday. 125 W. Congress St. ℭ **912/447-6952.**

The Rail   Not as aggressively noisy as Club One (see below), the Rail manages to be sophisticated and welcoming of divergent lifestyles. Its name acknowledges the 19th-century day laborers who used to congregate nearby every morning in hopes of being hired for a job on the local railway. Today you can "work the rail" in much more comfortable circumstances among some of Savannah's most engaging writers, artists, and eccentrics. Tavern-meisters Trina Marie Brown (from Los Angeles) and Melissa Swanson (from Connecticut) serve snack-style food, but most folks just drink and chat. 405 W. Congress St. ℭ **912/238-1311.**

Six Pence Pub   You can drop into this authentic-looking English pub for a selection of pub grub, including English fare along with homemade soups, salads, and sandwiches. On Sunday, an ale-and-mushroom pie is featured. Drinks are discounted during happy hour Monday to Friday 5 to 7pm. On Friday and Saturday, live music is offered, ranging from beach music to contemporary to jazz. It's open Sunday 12:30 to 10pm, Friday and Saturday 11:30am to 1am, and Monday to Thursday 11:30am to midnight. 245 Bull St. ℭ **912/233-3156.**

Wet Willie's   Few other nightspots in Savannah seem to revel so voluptuously in the effects produced by 190-proof grain alcohol. If you're hoping to get fall-down drunk, in a setting that evokes the more sociable aspects of an ongoing college-level fraternity/sorority bash, this is the place for you. When it's busy, it's loaded with the young, the nubile, and the sexually accessible—a worthy pickup joint if you're straight and not particularly squeamish. If you aren't sure what to order, consider such neon-colored headspinners as a Call-a-Cab, a Polar Cappuccino, a Monkey Shine, or a Shock Treatment. Karaoke is the venue every Monday and Tuesday night; otherwise it's something of a free-for-all with a Southern accent. Open Monday to Thursday 11am to 1am, Friday and Saturday 11am to 2am, and Sunday 12:30pm to 1am. 101 E. River St. ✆ 912/233-5650.

GAY & LESBIAN BARS

Club One   Club One defines itself as the premier gay bar in a town priding itself on a level of decadence that falls somewhere between New Orleans' and Key West's, and it's the hottest and most amusing spot in town. Patrons include lesbians and gays from the coastal islands; visiting urbanites; and cast and crew of whatever film is being shot in Savannah at the time (Demi Moore and Bruce Willis showed up here in happier times). There's also likely to be a healthy helping of voyeurs who've read *Midnight in the Garden of Good and Evil.*

You pay your admission at the door, showing ID if the attendant asks for it. Wander through the street-level dance bar, trek down to the basement-level video bar for a (less noisy) change of venue, and (if your timing is right) climb one floor above street level for a view of the drag shows. There, a bevy of black and white *artistes* lip-synch the hits of Tina Turner, Gladys Knight, and Bette Midler. It's open Monday to Saturday 5pm to 3am and Sunday 5pm to 2am. Shows are nightly at 10:30pm and 1am. 1 Jefferson St. ✆ 912/232-0200. Cover (after 9:30pm) $10 for those 18–20, $5 for those 21 and older.

Chuck's Bar   Most of the bars along Savannah's River Street are mainstream affairs, attracting goodly numbers of tourists, some of whom drink staggering amounts of booze and who seem almost proud of how rowdy they can get. In deliberate contrast, Chuck's usually attracts local members of Savannah's counterculture, including lots of gay folk, who rub elbows in a tuck-away corner of a neighborhood rarely visited by locals. The setting is a dark and shadowy 19th-century warehouse, lined with bricks, just a few steps from the Jefferson Street ramp leading down to the riverfront. Open

Monday to Saturday from 6pm to 3am. 305 Wet River St. ℂ **912/ 232-1005.**

Faces   Regulars sometimes refer to this neighborhood bar as the gay Cheers of Savannah. There's a pool table in back, and the unstudied decor includes battered ceiling beams, semirusted license plates, and an utter lack of concern about decorative fashion. Its provenance goes back to 1817, when it was a tavern. If you detect that the dialogues here might be a bit more insightful than the norm, part of it might be due to ownership by a licensed psychologist. Hours are Monday to Saturday 11am to 3am and Sunday 12:30pm to 2:30am. 17 Lincoln St. ℂ **912/233-3520.**

DINNER CRUISES

The *Savannah River Queen,* a replica of the boats that once plied this waterway, is a 350-passenger vessel operated by the River Street Riverboat Co., 9 E. River St. (ℂ **912/232-6404**). It offers a 2-hour cruise with a prime rib or fish dinner and live entertainment. Reservations are necessary. The fare is $35.95 for adults and $22.95 for children 11 and under. Departures are usually daily at 7pm, but the schedule might be curtailed in the colder months.

10 A Side Trip to Tybee Island

For more than 150 years, **Tybee Island** has lured those who wanted to go swimming, sailing, fishing, and picnicking. Pronounced "Tie-bee," an Euchee Indian word for "salt," the island offers 5 miles of unspoiled sandy beaches, only 14 miles east of Savannah. From Savannah, take U.S. 80 until you reach the ocean.

The **Tybee Island Visitors Center** (ℂ **800/868-BEACH** or 912/786-5444) provides complete information if you're planning to spend some time on the island, as opposed to a day trip. If you're interested in daily or weekly rentals of a bedroom condo or beach house (one or two bedrooms), contact **Tybee Beach Rentals,** P.O. Box 1440, Tybee Island, GA 31328 (ℂ **800/755-8562** or 912/786-8805).

Consisting of 5 square miles, Tybee was once called the "Playground of the Southeast," hosting millions of beach-loving visitors from across the country. In the 1880s it was a popular dueling spot. In the early 1900s, Tybrisa Pavilion, on the island's south end, became one of the major summer entertainment pavilions in the South. Some of the best-known bands, including those of Benny

Goodman, Guy Lombardo, Tommy Dorsey, and Cab Calloway, played here. It burned down in 1967 and was never rebuilt.

Over Tybee's salt marshes and sand dunes have flown the flags of pirates and Spaniards, the English and the French, and the Confederate States of America. A path on the island leads to a clear pasture where John Wesley, founder of the Methodist church, knelt and declared his faith in the new land.

Fort Screven, on the northern strip, began as a coastal artillery station and evolved into a training camp for countless troops in both world wars. Remnants of the wartime installations can still be seen. Also in the area is the **Tybee Museum,** housed in what was one of the fort's batteries. Displayed is a collection of photographs, memorabilia, art, and dioramas depicting Tybee from the time the Native Americans inhabited the island through World War II. Across the street is the **Tybee Lighthouse,** built in 1742 and the third-oldest lighthouse in America. It's 154 feet tall, and if you're fit you can climb 178 steps to the top. From the panoramic deck you get a sense of "the length and breadth of the marshes," as related in the Sidney Lanier poem "The Marshes of Glynn."

For information about the museum and lighthouse, call ✆ **912/ 786-5801.** Both the museum and the lighthouse are open April to September, daily 9am to 6pm; off-season hours are Monday and Wednesday to Friday 7am to 4pm and Saturday and Sunday 9am to 4pm. Adults pay $4; seniors 62 and older, $2; and children 6 to 15, $3. Kids 5 and under enter free. There are picnic tables here, and access to the beach is easy.

Tybee Marine Center, in the 14th Street parking lot (✆ **912/ 786-5917**), has aquariums with species indigenous to the coast of southern Georgia. Also on display are the usual cast of marine mammals, sharks, and other creatures. Hours are Monday to Saturday 9am to 4pm and Sunday 1 to 4pm. Admission is $1.

And no trip would be complete without a wonderful seafood lunch or dinner. The **Crab Shack at Chimney Creek,** 40 Estill Hammock Rd. (✆ **912/786-9857;** open year-round), advertises itself as "where the elite eat in their bare feet." Your lunch or dinner might've arrived just off the boat, having been swimming happily in the sea only an hour or so ago. Fat crab is naturally the specialty. It's most often preferred in cakes or can be blended with cheese and seasonings. Boiled shrimp is another popular item. Kids delight in selecting their crabs from a tank. A Low Country boil (a medley of seafood) is a family favorite, and the jukebox brings back the 1950s.

Index

See also Accommodations and Restaurant indexes below.

FROMMER'S® COMPLETE TRAVEL GUIDES

FROMMER'S® DOLLAR-A-DAY GUIDES

FROMMER'S® PORTABLE GUIDES

FROMMER'S® NATIONAL PARK GUIDES

FROMMER'S® MEMORABLE WALKS

Chicago
London

New York
Paris

San Francisco

FROMMER'S® GREAT OUTDOOR GUIDES

Arizona & New Mexico
New England

Northern California
Southern New England

Vermont & New Hampshire

SUZY GERSHMAN'S BORN TO SHOP GUIDES

Born to Shop: France
Born to Shop: Hong Kong,
  Shanghai & Beijing

Born to Shop: Italy
Born to Shop: London

Born to Shop: New York
Born to Shop: Paris

FROMMER'S® IRREVERENT GUIDES

Amsterdam
Boston
Chicago
Las Vegas
London

Los Angeles
Manhattan
New Orleans
Paris
Rome

San Francisco
Seattle & Portland
Vancouver
Walt Disney World
Washington, D.C.

FROMMER'S® BEST-LOVED DRIVING TOURS

Britain
California
Florida
France

Germany
Ireland
Italy

New England
Scotland
Spain

HANGING OUT™ GUIDES

Hanging Out in England
Hanging Out in Europe

Hanging Out in France
Hanging Out in Ireland

Hanging Out in Italy
Hanging Out in Spain

THE UNOFFICIAL GUIDES®

Bed & Breakfasts and Country
  Inns in:
    California
    New England
    Northwest
    Rockies
    Southeast
Beyond Disney
Branson, Missouri
California with Kids
Chicago
Cruises
Disneyland

Florida with Kids
Golf Vacations in the
  Eastern U.S.
The Great Smokey &
  Blue Ridge Mountains
Inside Disney
Hawaii
Las Vegas
London
Mid-Atlantic with Kids
Mini Las Vegas
Mini-Mickey
New England & New York
  with Kids

New Orleans
New York City
Paris
San Francisco
Skiing in the West
Southeast with Kids
Walt Disney World
Walt Disney World for
  Grown-ups
Walt Disney World for Kids
Washington, D.C.
World's Best Diving Vacations

SPECIAL-INTEREST TITLES

Frommer's Adventure Guide to Australia & New
  Zealand
Frommer's Adventure Guide to Central America
Frommer's Adventure Guide to India & Pakistan
Frommer's Adventure Guide to South America
Frommer's Adventure Guide to Southeast Asia
Frommer's Adventure Guide to Southern Africa
Frommer's Britain's Best Bed & Breakfasts and
  Country Inns
Frommer's France's Best Bed & Breakfasts and
  Country Inns
Frommer's Italy's Best Bed & Breakfasts and Country
  Inns
Frommer's Caribbean Hideaways

Frommer's Exploring America by RV
Frommer's Gay & Lesbian Europe
Frommer's The Moon
Frommer's New York City with Kids
Frommer's Road Atlas Britain
Frommer's Road Atlas Europe
Frommer's Washington, D.C., with Kids
Frommer's What the Airlines Never Tell You
Israel Past & Present
The New York Times' Guide to Unforgettable
  Weekends
Places Rated Almanac
Retirement Places Rated